LAW
ENFORCEMENT
A G E N C I E S

FEDERAL
BUREAU OF
INVESTIGATION

LAW ENFORCEMENT AGENCIES

Bomb Squad

Border Patrol

Federal Bureau of Investigation

The Secret Service

SWAT Teams

The Texas Rangers

LAW
ENFORCEMENT
A G E N C I E S

FEDERAL
BUREAU OF
INVESTIGATION

Edward R. Ricciuti

CHELSEA HOUSE
PUBLISHERS
An imprint of Infobase Publishing

FEDERAL BUREAU OF INVESTIGATION

Chelsea House
An imprint of Infobase Publishing
132 West 31st Street
New York NY 10001

Library of Congress Cataloging-in-Publication Data

Ricciuti, Edward R.
Federal Bureau of Investigation / Edward R. Ricciuti. -- 1st ed.
p. cm. — (Law enforcement agencies)
Includes bibliographical references and index.
ISBN-13: 978-1-60413-636-4 (hardcover : alk. paper)
ISBN-10: 1-60413-636-7 (hardcover : alk. paper) 1. United States. Federal
Bureau of Investigation—Juvenile literature. 2. Criminal investigation—
United States—Juvenile literature. I. Title.
HV8144.F43R53′2010   363.250973—dc22
2010030397

Chelsea House books are available at special discounts when purchased in bulk quantities for businesses, associations, institutions, or sales promotions. Please call our Special Sales Department in New York at (212) 967-8800 or (800) 322-8755.

You can find Chelsea House on the World Wide Web at http://www.chelseahouse.com

Text design and composition by Erika K. Arroyo
Cover design by Keith Trego
Cover printed by Bang Printing, Brainerd, Minn.
Book printed and bound by Bang Printing, Brainerd, Minn.
Date printed: December 2010

Printed in the United States of America

10 9 8 7 6 5 4 3 2 1

This book is printed on acid-free paper.

All links and Web addresses were checked and verified to be correct at the time of publication. Because of the dynamic nature of the Web, some addresses and links may have changed since publication and may no longer be valid.

Contents

Introduction

On July 26, 2008, the Federal Bureau of Investigation (FBI) marked its 100th anniversary as a crime fighting and national security agency dedicated to protecting the United States. During that time, the FBI has developed from a small group of bank examiners and labor-law investigators into one of the world's premier law enforcement and intelligence agencies. The mission of the FBI, according to the agency's official description, "is to uphold the law through the investigation of violations of federal criminal law; to protect the United States from foreign intelligence and terrorist activities; to provide leadership and law enforcement assistance to federal, state, local, and international agencies; and to perform these responsibilities in a manner that is responsive to the needs of the public and is faithful to the Constitution of the United States."

That statement covers considerable ground and, indeed, the FBI's mission is broad. In an age of international terrorism, it is still expanding. This book provides a primer on the FBI—what it was, what it is, and what it does. It will look at the evolving role of the FBI since its founding and how the agency continues to change in response to new challenges. The ways in which the priorities are identified by the agency will be described, as will the differences between the responsibilities of the FBI and other federal agencies.

More than 65 federal agencies have law enforcement officers authorized to carry firearms and make arrests under various federal laws. The total number of these officers that serve is at least 105,000. The largest employer of federal officers is U.S. Customs and Border Protection, with more than 28,000 officers. Second is the Federal Bureau of Prisons, with about 15,000 officers. Third is the FBI, which employees about 13,000, known as "special agents."[1]

The Federal Bureau of Investigation seal is displayed at the FBI Headquarters in Washington, D.C. *(Getty Images)*

Of all federal law enforcement agencies, the FBI is perhaps the best known, partly because federal law makes it the lead agency in investigating many different types of crime, and also because it has a massive, ongoing public relations program. The FBI's emphasis on keeping the public aware of its activities carries on a tradition started by the man who directed it for most of its century-plus existence, J. Edgar Hoover.

It was not until the 1930s, however, that the FBI emerged as a significant player among law enforcement agencies. Before that, it was something of a stepchild in the federal law enforcement establishment. Its agents were not even authorized to carry firearms. Today, the agency is equipped with high-tech scientific equipment and computer systems that would seem like science fiction to agents of the FBI's early days. At the same time, agents must maintain their ability to conduct the type of tenacious, old-fashioned investigations that made the FBI famous in the past. In addition, the FBI must continually adapt and change to meet challenges that continue to emerge on the national and international scene.

This book examines the FBI, starting in its earliest days and then focusing on its main areas of activity, ranging from international terrorism and organized crime to mortgage fraud and human trafficking. It looks at major cases, major changes in the way the FBI operates and the key tools that the agency uses to keep up with its mission.

Chapter 1, "This Is Your FBI," provides an overview of the FBI. It describes the agency, its structure, and what it does. Other topics include national security priorities, criminal priorities, crime prevention services for other agencies, and the legal framework under which the FBI operates.

Chapter 2, "The FBI's Century," surveys the history of the FBI, setting the stage for subjects described in later chapters. Covering major events in FBI history, the chapter discusses the development of the FBI from its inception to what it is today.

Chapter 3, "The FBI Laboratory: Science Battles Crime," describes how the FBI uses science against criminals and terrorists in the United States and abroad.

Chapter 4, "World War II," covers the days of World War II and how the FBI thwarted enemies who tried to wage war inside the United States.

Chapter 5, "Cold War Espionage," describes FBI activities during the Cold War era, including infamous cases such as that of the Rosenbergs, who stole secrets that helped the Soviets build the atom bomb.

Chapter 6, "Organized Crime," looks at how the FBI fights organized crime, a problem against which it has scored many victories but continues to emerge under new guises.

Chapter 7, "Desperados, Killers, and Kidnappers," examines violent crime, the ways it changes, the ways it stays the same, and what the FBI has done and continues to do to fight it.

Chapter 8, "Crime in High Places," delves into the world of white-collar crime and political corruption, which are as deadly to society in their own way as violent crime.

Chapter 9, "Protecting Civil Rights," describes how the FBI has emerged as the federal government's enforcer of civil rights violations, including the agency's history of battling racist groups such as the Ku Klux Klan (KKK) and its modern-day human trafficking investigations.

Chapter 10, "Terrorism," follows the FBI as it fights 21st-century domestic and international terrorism, including a newer brand of terrorism known as "special-interest terrorism."

This Is Your FBI

One of the most popular action series on radio during the years immediately after World War II featured dramatizations of famous FBI cases. *This Is Your FBI* aired on the American Broadcasting Company (ABC) from April 1945 to January 1953. FBI Director J. Edgar Hoover, a genius at promoting himself and his bureau, gave the program's producers access to FBI files and described it as "the finest dramatic program on the air."

The FBI and its exploits have always provided exciting material for fact and fiction that grabs the public's imagination. *This Is Your FBI* was only one of many programs about the agency during the heyday of radio. Due to the war and the FBI's campaigns against the sensational criminals of the 1930s, programs about the bureau and its agents were among the most popular radio action shows. Fascination with the FBI continues in the mass media, even if it is not always realistic—agents Fox Mulder and Dana Scully investigate the paranormal and far-out events in *The X-Files*; an FBI agent handles a hostage situation in *The Negotiator*; and after an eight-year run, *The FBI Files* still has reruns on television.

The amount of attention showered on the FBI by the mass media makes sense. For more than a century, it has been a major player in American history. The FBI is regularly in the news because of its involvement in some of the nation's most high-profile national security and criminal issues. Usually, the news is positive for the FBI and the nation. At times, the FBI—like any other organization—has botched the job, such as the flawed operation at Ruby Ridge in August 1992. While confronting white separatist Randy Weaver, agents, to use the words of FBI Director Louis J. Freeh before the U.S. Senate, "overreacted."[1] Weaver's wife and son, and a U.S. marshal ended up dead. Although mistakes by the FBI—and law enforcement in general—make for sensational headlines, they are the exception rather than the rule. The FBI can make a legitimate claim to being one of the world's premier law enforcement agencies.

MISCONCEPTIONS ABOUT THE FBI

Despite the FBI's high profile, there are many misconceptions on the part of the general public about what the FBI does and does not do. To correct false impressions, the FBI's Web site even provides a list of "The Top Ten Myths in FBI History." One involves the so-called X-Files (as portrayed in the television show of the same name), which the FBI says it does not have "squirreled away"[2] anywhere. The adventures of fictional agents Scully and Mulder to the contrary, the FBI says it does not investigate the supernatural or paranormal. On the other hand, it does have files on unusual happenings, such as UFO reports and mutilation of cattle and other domestic animals, often attributed to Satanists. The FBI says it keeps these files for the simple reason that people have reported them. If a violation of federal law may be involved, a seemingly supernatural incident may be investigated, but only for that reason.

Another misconception cited by the FBI is that there were no minority agents during the tenure of director J. Edgar Hoover, who ran the FBI for much of its existence. The FBI was hardly ahead of its time in providing equal career opportunities to all Americans, but it did employ some minority agents. Agent James Amos was a well-known black agent in New York from 1921 to 1953. Hispanic agent Manuel Sorola served during the 1940s. Today, more than 2,000 agents qualify as minority group members. In total, as of March 31, 2009, the FBI employed 14,005 women and 7,749 minorities.

Perhaps the most durable myth about the FBI is that Elliot Ness was an FBI agent. Ness was leader of the famed lawmen of the Prohibition Era called "the Untouchables," who received their name because they

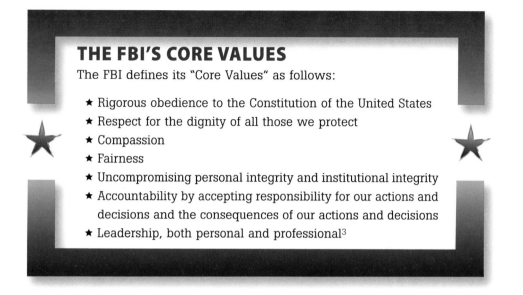

THE FBI'S CORE VALUES

The FBI defines its "Core Values" as follows:

★ Rigorous obedience to the Constitution of the United States
★ Respect for the dignity of all those we protect
★ Compassion
★ Fairness
★ Uncompromising personal integrity and institutional integrity
★ Accountability by accepting responsibility for our actions and decisions and the consequences of our actions and decisions
★ Leadership, both personal and professional[3]

could not be bribed by bootleggers and other criminals. Although he worked for J. Edgar Hoover for about a month, Ness was actually an agent for the U.S. Treasury Department.

THE FBI AND ITS MISSION

The FBI is the main investigative arm of the U.S. Department of Justice, which is supervised by the attorney general of the United States. Its main job is investigation of crimes that fall under its authority. It also provides an immense amount of assistance and training to other law enforcement agencies, both nationally and even internationally.

The official description of the FBI's mission today is "To protect and defend the United States against terrorist and foreign intelligence threats, to uphold and enforce criminal laws of the United States, and to provide leadership and criminal justice services to federal, state, municipal, and international agencies and partners." The "laws of the United States" refer to federal laws enacted by the U.S. Congress, not those instituted by state or local governments. Some exceptions exist. The FBI can be called upon, for example, when a state law enforcement officer is murdered or when serial killings occur. Over 200 categories of federal law come under the FBI's investigative authority. Federal law gives the FBI authority to investigate federal crimes not exclusively assigned to another federal agency. The Drug Enforcement Agency (DEA), for example, has a single mission—enforcement of drug laws. It is the lead agency for drug crime but the FBI shares jurisdiction with it. The Bureau of Alcohol, Tobacco, Firearms, and Explosives (ATF) has primary responsibility for investigating violations of federal firearms laws and of arsons and bombings not furthering terrorist causes, but the FBI has the authority to investigate cases involving bombings of property used in interstate commerce or cases involving terrorism. Some crimes, such as kidnapping, are specifically assigned to the FBI.

Some people confuse the jobs of the FBI and the Central Intelligence Agency (CIA). The CIA is not a law enforcement agency. Its mission is to collect and analyze information about adversaries and potential enemies of the United States. At the direction of the president, the CIA also conducts covert operations in the name of national interest, a practice that has generated controversy, rumors, misconceptions, and debate over the years. The CIA cannot collect information on what the law calls "U.S. persons," which includes citizens, corporations, resident aliens, and legal immigrants, wherever they live.

The FBI routinely works to detect spying undertaken by foreign interests in the United States. Unlike the CIA, however, it cannot engage in or investigate spying overseas.

Of the dozens of federal agencies with law enforcement powers, the FBI has the broadest jurisdiction. FBI agents have the authority to make arrests for federal crimes within the United States and its territories. Congress may authorize the power of arrest on foreign soil, if the foreign government agrees.

The FBI does not bring charges against criminal suspects; that is the job of the U.S. attorneys, who support the attorney general. Results of FBI investigations are handed over the federal prosecutors. They review the evidence, and then decide whether or not to go ahead with the case.

To say that the FBI is a very busy agency puts it mildly. Here are some figures about the FBI's daily workload, reported in 2009:[4]

- 7,000 terrorist leaders investigated in the United States
- More than 40 intelligence reports produced
- 12,000 fugitives from justice sought
- More than 70,000 fingerprint submissions processed

- More than 74,000 names checked in the national database
- Processed about 5.5 million transactions—such as running license plates—through the National Crime Information Center (NCIC), an index of criminal information
- Investigated 30 allegations of fraud relating to activities in the wake of Hurricane Katrina
- Investigated about 450 pending environmental crimes cases, half of which involve the Clean Water Act

It takes a lot of manpower to perform all of that work. As of March 31, 2009, the FBI had 31,891 employees, including 13,075 special agents. Others include staffers ranging from clerks to scientists and information specialists. All employees undergo a thorough screening and background check because they must qualify for and maintain a top-secret security clearance.

Special agents are chosen from a pool of applicants who are U.S. citizens between 23 and 37 years of age with at least a bachelor's degree from an accredited, four-year resident program at a college or university. Traditionally, the FBI favored candidates with backgrounds in law enforcement, accounting, or law. Today, however, people with expertise in other fields, such as computers, intelligence, languages, and the sciences, are also sought. Since the September 11, 2001, terrorist attacks, hundreds of intelligence analysts, linguists, and surveillance specialists have been hired, and the effort to hire more specialists and agents continues. Prospective agents train for 20 weeks at the FBI Academy in Quantico, Virginia. As part of their training, new special agents visit the U.S. Holocaust Memorial Museum to see what can happen when law enforcement breaks down and fails to protect individuals.

The top person in the FBI is its director, who is appointed by the president and confirmed by the Senate. On October 15, 1976, Congress passed Public Law 94-503, which limits the term of an FBI director to 10 years. The law was designed largely to prevent an FBI director from amassing the power that was wielded by former director Hoover, who remained in office for almost 50 years.

The current director is Robert S. Mueller III. He was confirmed on August 2, 2001, giving him barely enough time to settle down in his office before the attacks of September 11 shook the world. He had been a U.S. attorney and then assistant attorney general in charge of the Department of Justice's Criminal Division. Formerly a practicing lawyer with a graduate degree in international relations, Mueller was also an officer in the U.S. Marine Corps.

FBI OPERATIONS

FBI operations cost a vast amount of money, which must be approved by Congress. The FBI received $6.4 billion for 2008. FBI operations worldwide are coordinated from headquarters in the J. Edgar Hoover Building in Washington, D.C. The FBI has other facilities outside Washington, including its crime laboratory, Criminal Justice Information Services Division, the academy, and field offices across the country. High-tech computer centers are located in several cities. The day-to-

WRITTEN IN THE LAW

The powers of the FBI are written into laws passed by Congress. Together, they give the FBI the authority to investigate crimes within its jurisdiction. The agency's basic authority comes under Title 28 of the U.S. Code, Section 533, which authorizes the U.S. attorney general to appoint officials to detect and prosecute crimes against the United States. Title 18, Section 3052 of the code authorizes special agents to make arrests, carry firearms, and serve warrants. Title 18, Section 3107 gives special agents power to make seizures under warrants for violation of federal statutes, or laws. Other congressional laws explicitly allow the FBI to violate certain laws. The 1946 federal Atomic Energy Act, for example, gave the FBI the responsibility for protecting secret nuclear technology. Other laws gave the FBI specific authority over cases involving kidnapping and robbery of banks covered by the Federal Deposit Insurance Corporation. Other responsibilities of the FBI, including collection of fingerprint cards and identification records and training of other police officers, fall under the Code of Federal Regulations, Title 28, Section 0.85.

FBI Director Robert Mueller speaks during a news conference in June 2008 at the Department of Justice in Washington, D.C., regarding a nationwide crackdown on incidents of mortgage fraud that have contributed to the country's housing crisis. *(AP Photo/ Jose Luis Magana)*

day investigations and other basic work of the FBI is done out of its 56 field offices and their 400 satellites. Stationed in these offices are most of the agents who carry out the mission of the FBI. Most field offices are headed by a special agent in charge. The largest field offices, in Washington, D.C., Los Angeles, and New York City, are run by assistant directors in charge.

The FBI must maintain an international presence, especially in the current age of international terrorism. Seventy-five international offices, known as Legal Attaches (Legats), and their sub-offices are scattered around the globe to coordinate work with intelligence and law enforcement agencies in 200 countries. FBI responsibilities overseas were extended during the 1980s when Congress passed so called long-arm laws, which permit the U.S. government to charge individuals who attack U.S. interests abroad with criminal violations and return them to the United States for trial. Agents are dispatched to the scene of international attacks and disasters, such as the July 2005 bombings in London and May 2003 bombings in Saudi Arabia. Agents also work with and train law enforcement and counterterrorism officers in Iraq and Afghanistan. They often work in conjunction with agents from other agencies, such as the U.S. Secret Service and U.S. Department of State.

Historically, there have been times when law enforcement agencies—at all levels and including the FBI—engage in competition for the limelight and for funding. This still occurs, but it is much less prevalent than in the past, largely because the threat of domestic and international terrorism has made cooperation necessary for the nation's survival.

The FBI has endured its share of criticism regarding cooperation (or lack thereof), but it has taken significant steps to solve the problem. An important move occurred on December 4, 2001, when the FBI created its Office of Law Enforcement Coordination. Its function is to improve coordination and sharing of information with other agencies, such as the exchange of fingerprint and arrest information. Although routine, such cooperation sometimes does not go smoothly in some cases, a problem that the coordination office is designed to eliminate.

A significant area of cooperation is the FBI's Joint Terrorism Task Force (JTTF). In JTTFs, which have been established at field offices, agents and officers from several federal, state, and local agencies are deployed alongside FBI agents for counterterrorism operations and investigations. These task forces include personnel from agencies such as sheriff's departments, state police, municipal police, the U.S. Marshals Service, U.S. Immigration and Customs Enforcement (ICE), and the Internal Revenue Service.

The task forces have gone a long way toward easing resentment by local and state agencies over alleged takeovers of investigations by the FBI. More often than not, all agencies involved pool their efforts. The FBI can help local departments by notifying them if any new fingerprints matched to a suspect on the run turn up. Information on terrorism is shared by the FBI through its Terrorist Threat Integration Center.

Testifying on the FBI budget before the U.S. House Judiciary Committee on May 20, 2009, FBI Director Mueller described the present-day FBI as a "national security service."[5] Since the attacks of September 11, he noted, counterterrorism has been the agency's top priority. Counterintelligence and cybersecurity follow as number two and three on the FBI's priority list, respectively.

Economic crime has also gained importance among FBI priorities. Mueller stressed this fact in his testimony before Congress only weeks

FBI PRIORITIES

The FBI names its present priorities as the following:[6]

★ Protect the United States from terrorist attack
★ Protect the United States against foreign intelligence operations and espionage
★ Protect the United States against cyber-based attacks and high-technology crimes
★ Combat public corruption at all levels
★ Protect civil rights
★ Combat transnational/national criminal organizations and enterprises
★ Combat major white-collar crime
★ Combat significant violent crime
★ Support federal, state, local, and international partners
★ Upgrade technology to successfully perform the FBI's mission

Two FBI agents escort a suspect in a mortgage-fraud scheme after he was taken into custody in New York in October 2009. *(Brendan McDermid/Reuters/Corbis)*

before the sensational arrest of financier Bernard Madoff in a huge fraud case. With the recession and housing crisis underway, the FBI increased its efforts to root out mortgage fraud, which began to show a significant increase in 2008.

In combating mortgage fraud, the FBI used tactics similar to those used to obtain evidence in cases involving spies, terrorists, and violent gangsters: undercover operations and wiretaps. Investigative techniques of this sort sometimes result in the arrest of criminals while they are committing crimes.

Wiretapping private telephones can be a controversial issue if it violates individual rights to privacy. It is, by any account, one of the FBI's most sensitive techniques. Federal laws—contained in Title 18, Section 2516 of the U.S. Code—strictly control its use, which is not nearly as frequent as many people suspect. Wiretapping is mostly used as a weapon against extremely serious crimes. The code requires law enforcement officers to establish probable cause that wiretaps may provide evidence of a serious violation, a felony, of federal law. The argument that wiretaps are necessary is provided to a federal judge. The judge then decides whether their use is warranted. The use of wiretaps without a court order is a felony.

The FBI's Century

The Federal Bureau of Investigation celebrated its centennial in 2008. During its first century, it developed from a handful of agents with limited powers to what many people see as the premier enforcement agency in the nation. The FBI's exploits in fighting crime and protecting national security are legendary, but an unusual fact about its beginnings largely escapes notice: Its founding father was the grandnephew of French Emperor Napoleon Bonaparte. The FBI traces its origin to an order issued by Charles Joseph Bonaparte, who was appointed U.S. attorney general by President Theodore Roosevelt. A native of Baltimore, Maryland, and graduate of Harvard University and Harvard Law School, Bonaparte helped Roosevelt break up trusts that had unfairly monopolized the nation's commerce.

When Bonaparte was appointed, the U.S. attorney general had no investigators under his authority. He had to borrow them from other agencies such as the Secret Service, which annoyed Bonaparte to no end; in effect, the Justice Department depended on what amounted to "renting" personnel from other agencies. Congress solved this problem by outlawing the practice. So, in 1908, Bonaparte ordered the formation of a force of 34 permanent investigators in the Department of Justice. Most of them had been involved in examining banks, investigating violations of labor laws, and similar nonviolent offenses. Now Bonaparte had his own "corps of special agents." Their job was to handle investigations into about 20 different types of cases, most of which were not particularly glamorous, such as antitrust issues and copyright violations, but not bank fraud. The FBI began with that small group of agents, which in 1909 was named the Department of Investigation.

BEGINNING TO GROW

As the power of the federal government increased with the passage of time, so did that of the Justice Department and its investigators. New

Charles Joseph Bonaparte, American attorney general and secretary of the Navy, was instrumental in creating the Department of Investigation, which later became the Federal Bureau of Investigation. *(Corbis)*

laws extended the department's authority. The 1910 White-Slave Traffic Act, for example, placed interstate prostitution under the jurisdiction of the new bureau, and the 1910 Dyer Act authorized it to investigate interstate auto theft.

By the time the United States entered World War 1, in 1917, the bureau had 300 employees. After a convoluted process of arguments and debate between different agencies during the war, President Woodrow Wilson gave them a new mission: investigating espionage, sabotage, and sedition, and investigating violation of military draft laws. Despite this expansion of power, the bureau was still not counted among the major players in law enforcement. Agents could investigate crimes on their own, but they depended on members of other agencies to make actual arrests. Moreover, except in unusual cases, they were not authorized to carry firearms.

In 1919 Congress passed the Eighteenth Amendment to the U.S. Constitution, which banned the manufacture, transportation, and sale of alcohol. The era of Prohibition, a colorful but violent time, began. Bootlegging—the illegal making, transporting, and selling of alcohol— was rampant and made criminals and criminal organizations rich. The rise of the automobile made transporting illegal liquor much more efficient. Criminal gangs fought turf wars over control of illegal liquor sales. Guns blazed on the streets of American cities, much as they do today between warring street gangs. However, these activities were largely outside the jurisdiction of the FBI. Instead, U.S. marshals and Treasury Department agents spearheaded law enforcement efforts.

HOOVER TAKES CHARGE

Meanwhile, the bureau had internal problems. Its director, William J. Burns, was implicated in political scandals and massive misuse of power. He was forced to resign in 1924. A new director named J. Edgar Hoover took over. For almost a half century, he was the face of the FBI, although when he first took the helm, it was still called the Bureau of Investigation.

Hoover cleaned up the bureau by raising professional standards and adopting the most modern investigative techniques. He implemented the requirement that agents have a college degree, a revolutionary step at the time. He was convinced that recent scientific advances could benefit law enforcement. Accordingly, he established an Identification Division in 1924 to help law enforcement agencies throughout the nation track criminals by fingerprints, then a relatively new technique. Fascinated by science, in 1932 he created a forensics unit within the bureau that constituted the nation's first major crime laboratory.

Hoover cleaned out ineffective agents and people who had gotten jobs through political influence, reducing the number of agents from 441 to 339 in five years.[1]

J. Edgar Hoover, former director of the Federal Bureau of Investigation, works at his desk in his office in the Department of Justice Building in Washington, D.C., in September 1942. Hoover was in charge of the FBI for almost 50 years, becoming one of the most powerful men in the country along the way. *(AP Photo)*

J. EDGAR HOOVER

J. Edgar Hoover is perhaps the most recognizable figure in the history of American law enforcement. Hoover was actually a native Washingtonian, born in that city on New Year's Day, 1895. His youth is not well documented. After he received a law degree from George Washington University in 1917, he caught the eye of his superiors at the Justice Department, where he had found a job. World War I was on and he was quickly made head of the Enemy Aliens Registration Section. Within a few years, he had risen to head the Justice Department's General Intelligence Division, which had been established to investigate radicals and subversives. The government at the time was worried about radical socialists, Russian Bolsheviks, and anarchists. His men arrested several radicals who were deported to Russia. They also investigated and accosted many people who, it turned out, were innocent and in no way a danger to the nation. Hoover remained concerned about people he thought were dangerously radical for the rest of his career. It was later found that he had maintained a list

Despite modernization, Hoover's agency was a long way from the cutting-edge FBI of today. Its name was still the Bureau of Investigation and its jurisdiction was still relatively limited. All that changed after President Franklin Roosevelt took office in 1933 and immediately reorganized the Department of Justice. By then, the Bureau of Prohibition, which enforced the ban on alcohol, was under the Justice Department. Roosevelt placed it and the Bureau of Investigation under a new Justice Department arm, called the Division of Investigation, and placed Hoover in charge. A few months later, however, Congress repealed the Eighteenth Amendment, so the Bureau of Prohibition was no longer needed. Thus the only agency left within the Division of Investigation was the Bureau of Investigation.

Confusion reigned because other federal agencies had their own divisions of investigation. At Hoover's request, his bureau received its of thousands of Americans whose loyalties he thought suspect. Shortly after taking the helm of the intelligence division, President Calvin Coolidge named Hoover head of the Bureau of Investigation. He was only 29 years of age.

Hoover's word was law within the bureau, and he became one of the most powerful men in Washington. He hired and fired agents at will. He also kept files on politicians and other important people for possible use against them. After his death, critics accused him of many improprieties, ranging from misuse of power to harass civil rights leaders such as Martin Luther King, to strange sexual misbehavior.

Stories of "black bag jobs," or illegal searches, abounded and many probably were true. Hoover was idolized by large segments of the American public during most of his 48-year directorship. He maintained public relations machinery to boost his favorable image as the nation's number one crime fighter. And, in many ways, he was. For decades, Hoover *was* the FBI, and while shaping the FBI, he helped revolutionize modern law enforcement.

own name. On March 22, 1936, with the approval of Congress, Hoover's bureau was officially designated as the Federal Bureau of Investigation.

The FBI would soon have another name or, more accurately, a nickname: G-Men. The name, short for "government men," was applied to agents by gangsters who had become FBI targets. According to legend, the FBI got that name when the notorious Machine Gun Kelly was cornered and pleaded, "Don't shoot, G-Men."[2]

The violent crime of the 1920s had carried over to the 1930s. If anything, it had become even more widespread and deadly. The grueling hard times caused by the Great Depression turned some desperate people toward crime. It prompted others to idolize gangsters who robbed the banks that had foreclosed on their homes and businesses.

Organized crime and ethnic gangs—such as Al Capone's bootlegging syndicate in Chicago—had taken control of criminal enterprises in cities across the country. At the same time, Charles "Lucky" Luciano was uniting Italian-American gangs in New York City into what later became known as Cosa Nostra or the Mafia. In the countryside, especially the Midwest, outlaws such as Bonnie Parker and Clyde Barrow ran wild like the bandits of earlier years, except they rode in automobiles instead of on horses, and they carried machine guns rather than six-shooters. Most of the time, they outgunned the police in terms of firepower—the Thompson submachine gun was a popular weapon—and drove bigger, faster vehicles.

In response, in the early 1930s Congress passed several laws dealing with crime. These new laws vastly expanded the jurisdiction of the FBI to cover many crimes, such as interstate kidnapping. On top of this jurisdictional expansion, agents were authorized by Congress to go beyond pure investigation and make arrests—and, for the first time, to legally carry weapons. The sidearm issued was the .32 caliber Colt Pocket Positive, an easily concealed, snub-nosed revolver with a very short barrel. The introduction of weapons-carrying powers was prompted by the so-called Kansas City massacre. In June 1933 three police officers and one bureau agent escorting a prisoner through a Missouri train station were ambushed and killed by gangster Pretty Boy Floyd and his confederates. Although the agent was armed, he had no authority to bear a weapon.

New authority did not automatically transform the bureau into an elite crime-fighting unit. In fact, agents stumbled at times in their pursuit of top criminals. Perhaps their worst embarrassment came during a raid on a Wisconsin resort lodge, Little Bohemia.

On a Sunday morning in April 1934, agents received a tip that the notorious bank robber and jailbreak specialist John Dillinger, with his gang, were holed up in the lodge, a two-story building bordered by cabins on a lake. With him was another murderous gangster, Baby Face Nelson (Lester Joseph Gillis). Agents arrived at night, shivering in the chilly air. As they approached the lodge, three men came out and got into a car.

"Stop. Federal agents. Police. Stop," the agents shouted.[3] The men, who had turned on the car radio, did not hear the commands. Agents opened fire, killing the driver. He was not a gangster but a member of the Civilian Conservation Corps—a public work program for men during the Depression—who had been drinking at the lodge with his friends.

Hearing the commotion outside, Dillinger and his men let loose a volley of shots from the second floor of the lodge. In the confusion, they escaped out the back, but the ordeal was not over. Baby Face Nelson emerged, stole a car and, confronting agents, killed one, wounded another, and wounded a local policeman. The tragedy proved that FBI agents needed more training in many aspects of police work, including raw and violent shootouts with ruthless criminals. Hoover liked to hire agents who were logical thinkers, especially people trained in accounting and law. A third of the bureau's original agents, in fact, were bank examiners, and thus accountants by profession. A good investigator, however, does not necessarily make a good street cop. FBI agents did eventually track down and kill both Nelson and Dillinger. Their deaths went a long way toward bringing the FBI into the public limelight.

Few law enforcement agencies at the time offered formal training to peace officers. The FBI had started a training program in 1929 but it focused on classroom and technical courses, such as fingerprinting and collecting evidence. Physical training was confined to exercises on the rooftop of the Justice Department building.

In 1935 the FBI launched its Police Training School. It would become the FBI Academy at Quantico, Virginia, which trains not only FBI agents but also law enforcement personnel from all over the world. Because agents received their marksmanship training on firing ranges at the U.S. Marine Corps Base in Quantico, it was logical to use the city as a site for the academy. Today the academy is a modern facility that the FBI likes to call the "West Point of Law Enforcement."[4]

NEW RESPONSIBILITIES

By the mid-1930s, war clouds began to gather over the world. The FBI was called on to assume additional duties. Secretly, in 1939 President Roosevelt placed the FBI at the helm of homeland security, with help from the armed forces. The FBI was ordered by Roosevelt to probe the possibility that Nazi or Communist agents were bent on subversive action within the United States, including espionage and sabotage. A year later, on the eve of the United States' entry into World War II, the president ordered the FBI to gather foreign intelligence in Central and South America, where the Nazis had ongoing operations. Roosevelt

THE FBI SHIELD

Like the designs on the shields of medieval knights, the images on the FBI seal tell a story. The scales represent the scales of justice. The 13-star circle represents unity of purpose, like that of the original 13 states. The crown of laurel branches, similar to that used to decorate heroes in ancient times, represents honor and distinction. The branches contain 46 leaves, the number of states in the Union when the FBI was founded. The red stripes signify courage and strength while the white stands for truth and peace. The rough edges of the seal symbolize the challenges confronting the FBI, and its toughness. The motto of the FBI—"Fidelity, Bravery, Integrity"—was coined by W.H. Drane Lester, the editor of the FBI's in-house employee magazine, in 1935.[5]

had reason to worry—the Nazis were using Latin America as a staging ground for espionage, and Nazi spies were actually infiltrating the United States. In addition, Japan was successfully sending its own spies into the country.

The FBI's wartime work began in earnest in June 1940, when it formed a Special Intelligence Service Division (SIS). During the course of the war, the SIS discovered about 1,300 spies working for the Germans and Japanese; major spy and sabotage rings within the United States were uncovered and its participants arrested and prosecuted. (The SIS was disbanded once the Central Intelligence Agency was established in 1947.) About 50 of the spies were nabbed even before the United States entered the war. Not one act of sabotage directed by the Axis Powers occurred on U.S. soil during the war.

Expanded responsibilities required more manpower, and consequently FBI numbers grew from 2,400 agents and other employees in 1940 to 13,000 in 1944. While the FBI still focused energies on crime fighting, it had emerged as a major force for national security, which is of highest priority to the agency today.

THE COLD WAR

The national security capabilities developed during World War II helped the FBI cope with a new kind of war that followed. When the Soviet Union's "Iron Curtain" was drawn on Eastern Europe, the cold war between East and West began. The Soviet Union had planned ahead for the aftermath of World War II. While the Soviets were an ally to the United States against the Germans, they planted spies liberally in the United States, even in sensitive areas of the federal government. The Soviets also cultivated Communist and left-wing sympathizers among U.S. citizens.

Gradually, the FBI began to block Soviet penetration. This effort was helped by the U.S. Army Signal Corps, which began intercepting telegrams from Soviet spies even before World War II ended. Secret until 1995, this operation, called the Venona Project, enabled the FBI to crack a major spy case—that of Julius and Ethel Rosenberg—and a ring that passed on secrets about the atomic bomb to Moscow. The program was later picked up by the National Security Agency until it was terminated in 1980.

During the 1950s, the FBI managed to out many Soviet operatives. At the same time, a "red baiting" scare was sweeping the country, inspired by U.S. Senator Joseph R. McCarthy, a Wisconsin Republican. He held hearings that spawned widespread fears of Communist subversion. He smeared personal enemies and political opponents by inferring that they had Communist leanings. McCarthy and his tactics were eventually discredited. He was censured by the Senate and died at age 48 of liver disease, possibly brought on by alcoholism. Given that J. Edgar Hoover was an ardent anticommunist, he has been accused by some critics of cooperating in the senator's misdeeds.

FBI files do contain substantial correspondence between the two men, which is not unexpected given their positions. In one letter, McCarthy describes a threatening letter he received from a man in Oakland, California, who, the senator says, "sounds like a screwball." Whatever the relationship between the two men, McCarthy's excesses should not diminish the immense contributions of FBI agents to national security during the cold war.

CHANGING MISSIONS IN A CHANGING WORLD

The new priorities and missions of the FBI reflect major developments in the history of the United States. By the mid 1960s, passage of federal civil rights laws had given the FBI a central role in the federal government's efforts to ensure equal rights for all. Previously, the agency had frequently been handcuffed by a lack of jurisdiction when local officials turned a blind eye to violations of the civil rights of blacks and other minorities. Agency historians are fond of pointing out that the FBI actually has a long history of civil rights investigations. Several of its first agents who were not bank examiners were "peonage" investigators, whose field of expertise was abuse of laborers. Among the first major cases of the civil rights era were the Baptist church bombing in Birmingham, Alabama, in September 1963 and the murders of three civil rights workers in Mississippi about a year later. The latter case became known as Mississippi Burning after its case name, MIBURN.

Domestic terrorists such as the Weather Underground and the Symbionese Liberation Army occupied the FBI during the 1970s. By then, the FBI was undergoing even more changes. J. Edgar Hoover had died in office in 1972, and the agency had hardly recovered from Hoover's death when, five weeks later, the Watergate scandal exploded. FBI agents were prominent in the investigation and, it turned out, in leaking information about the probe to the press. In 2005 former FBI Deputy Director Mark Felt was identified as "Deep Throat," the code name given to a mysterious leaker by a *Washington Post* editor. The newspaper broke the story of the Nixon administration's burglary of Democratic National Committee headquarters in Washington's Watergate building. During the Watergate probe of illegal activities by the administration, the FBI was under great pressure from administration officials to rein in the investigation. Felt's boss, L. Patrick Gray, had been appointed acting director of the FBI after Hoover's death and was not yet confirmed when Watergate occurred. He later admitted that he was sympathetic to the administration and kept the administration informed on the investigation. Gray's actions damaged the FBI's image, even though agents came up with much of the evidence that broke the case and brought about Nixon's downfall.

The agency was further hurt by charges that some of its intelligence and surveillance activities went overboard, even to the point of infringing on the rights of individuals to privacy. Under Hoover, the FBI had monitored and investigated several public figures, including the Reverend Martin Luther King Jr. After public hearings on the issue, headed by Senator Frank Church, an Idaho Democrat, the FBI worked with the attorney general to bring the agency's domestic security operations well within constitutional rights.

Another investigation by the FBI of wrongdoing by public officials in cahoots with criminals was code-named ABSCAM. Revealed in 1980, it resulted in a U.S. senator and six congressmen, plus more than a dozen other corrupt officials and criminals, going to jail.

The investigation started in 1978 with the purpose of catching New York City crime figures suspected of dealing in stolen art. The FBI set up a false company in Long Island, called Abdul Enterprises, said to be owned by a wealthy Arab sheik and giving the operation its name (after "Abdul scam"). The "sheik" was in the market for valuable works of art. The criminals fell for the sting and the FBI recovered two paintings worth $1 million.

During the operation, the undercover agents were introduced to a host of criminals dealing in a wide range of illicit activities, including selling fake stocks and bonds worth millions of dollars. The probe led to Washington, D.C., when the agents asked their criminal contacts if, for a bribe, they could obtain political asylum in the United States for their boss, the "sheik." They also asked for other political favors to further the sheik's business interests. In 1981 separate trials brought convictions on bribery and conspiracy charges for Senator Harrison A. Williams of New Jersey, and five members of the House of Representatives: John Jenrett of South Carolina, Richard Kelly of Florida, Raymond Lederer of Pennsylvania, Michael Meyers of Pennsylvania, and Frank Thompson of New Jersey.

It was a major achievement for the FBI, but the operation had its critics. Questions were raised as to whether the agents illegally entrapped those convicted. Later court rulings upheld the convictions. However, the case did prompt the enactment of stronger guidelines for carrying out sting operations like ABSCAM.

With such high-profile cases coming one on the heels of the other, the FBI's efforts against organized crime often went unnoticed. Even so, the efforts continued. Passed by congress in 1970, the Racketeer Influenced and Corrupt Organizations Act (RICO) gave more legal muscle to go after organized crime by giving the FBI the power to prosecute organizations rather than only individuals. Every so often, the FBI's investigation of a major crime figure made the news, such as the 1992 conviction of Gambino family boss John Gotti on murder and several other charges. He landed in jail, where he remained until his death in 2002.

THE FBI IN A NEW CENTURY

Throughout its history, the FBI has evolved to meet new challenges. Depending on the times, priorities have involved a full spectrum of criminal activities, including gangsters, organized crime, public corruption, hate crimes, cyberattacks, white-collar fraud, and terrorism. No challenge or transformation has been more "far-reaching," in the agency's own words, than that posed by the terrorist attacks of September 11, 2001, and their legacy. "Even before the dust settled," says the FBI's Web site, "we had a new overriding mission to stop terrorists before they strike." The agency "needed to be more forward-leaning, more predictive, a step ahead of the next germinating threat."

During the first 75 years of its history, the terrorism faced by the FBI was mainly domestic and linked to larger criminal trends. Between World Wars I and II, this threat came primarily from right-wing extremists, such as fascist groups and the Ku Klux Klan; it then shifted to left-wing, socialist-oriented groups beginning in the 1950s and continuing into the 1980s. Prominent among them was the Weather Underground. A violent offshoot of the Students for a Democratic Society, which demanded social change, the Weather Underground planted bombs in several government installations, including, in January 1975, the U.S. State Department. In the early 1980s international terrorism—sponsored primarily by foreign states or organizations—began to impact U.S. interests overseas. It led to legislation that extended the FBI's responsibilities to cover terrorist threats originating outside the United States and its territories. The 1990s saw a new era of domestic and international terrorism. Terrorists sought to inflict massive and indiscriminate casualties upon civilian populations. This threat grew as terrorists began to seek out unconventional weapons and weapons of mass destruction. The 1990s also saw the rise of terrorism pursued by loosely affiliated extremists. They ranged from terrorists involved with domestic special interest causes to militants engaged in international jihad. These terrorism trends culminated with the September 11, 2001, attack that has set in motion an international effort to counter the global terrorist threat and elevated counterterrorism to the FBI's preeminent mission.

In his September 20, 2001, address to a joint session of Congress and the American people, President Bush assured his audience that in the present conflict with terrorism, violence would be met with "patient justice." The struggle against terrorism—especially that currently waged against Al-Qaeda—is one of endurance, and it is one in which the FBI is prepared to engage with unflagging persistence. The preeminent mission of protecting the United States from terrorist attack is changing the character of the FBI as a whole. However, the FBI continues investigating and prosecuting criminal acts. It can bring its expertise in criminal investigations to bear on terrorist activities, the dismantling of terrorist organizations, and, consequently, the prevention of future terrorist attacks. By combining a willingness to innovate with its traditional law enforcement responsibilities, the FBI continues to evolve in order to counter the varied forms of terrorism that threaten the interests and security of the United States.

The FBI has been forced by events at the beginning of the 21st century to strengthen its intelligence and counterterrorism capabilities in many new ways. It has begun its second century of operation by working with other law enforcement agencies in the United States and abroad to stop threats from terrorism, cybercrime, and other global dangers.

The FBI
Laboratory:
Science Battles
Crime

Harrington Fitzgerald Jr., a mental patient at the Pennsylvania veterans hospital, did not recognize the name on a card that came with a box of chocolates in November 1933. The handwritten note on the card said the candy was from "Bertha." Although he had no idea who "Bertha" was, Fitzgerald opened the box and ate the candy. A short time later, he was dead. The candy was poisoned.

Normally, local police would have investigated a poisoning. However, the hospital was a federal institution, so agents from the U.S. Bureau of Investigation were called in to investigate the case.

Suspicion quickly fell on the victim's sister, Sarah Hobart, who lived 100 miles away in Philadelphia. Agents obtained samples of her handwriting to compare it with the "Bertha" signature. The samples, along with the wrapper of the candy box, were sent to the bureau's brand new Technical Crime Laboratory, which had been founded only about a year before. When analyzed, however, the writing on the card did not match Hobart's samples.

The only scientist staffing the laboratory was Special Agent Charles Appel, a balding, unassuming man who had been an aviator in World

War I and was known for his painstaking investigative methods. After the failed handwriting match, he decided to try a different approach. The mailing label on the candy package had been printed by a manual typewriter, and agents found that Hobart's family had a typewriter, but it was not in their home. They tracked it to a repair shop. Analysis at the laboratory showed it was the machine that had typed the mailing label. Confronted, Hobart confessed to the murder. She was later ruled insane. The FBI often cites the Fitzgerald murder case as one of the first investigations conducted by its laboratory.[1] The FBI laboratory, located in Quantico, Virginia, is known worldwide for its use of forensic science, also known as forensics, to combat crime and terrorism.

In the law enforcement world, forensics is described as the use of the sciences and other fields of knowledge—art and accounting, for instance—to gather and evaluate evidence for use in a court of law. The evidence involved can be virtually anything connected with a case, from the appearance of a knife wound to the molecular makeup of a piece of metal. The sciences employed range from entomology (the study of insects) and geology to psychology and toxicology.

Forensic investigation starts at the scene of the crime, where evidence is recovered and, importantly, preserved. At this point, what is called the "chain of custody" begins. This term describes the timeline of documentation that keeps track of when and how evidence was gathered and the hands through which it passed for various purposes, such as storage and analysis. Every link in the chain is recorded to safeguard it against tampering or other means by which it could be compromised. After evidence is gathered, it eventually ends up in a forensics laboratory, popularly known as a crime lab. The FBI Laboratory is one of the most complete and sophisticated anywhere in the world.

THE LABORATORY BEGINS

When J. Edgar Hoover took over the leadership of the Bureau of Investigation, forensics laboratories were new to law enforcement. The world's first crime lab was only a few decades old. It had been founded in 1910 in Lyons, France, by Dr. Edmond Locard, a pathologist who talked the city police department into giving him two rooms for his new facility. Six years later, the Los Angeles Police Department established the first crime laboratory in the United States. Another was founded in Chicago by Colonel Calvin Goddard, a U.S. Army officer and expert in ballistics, the study of firearm and ammunition characteristics.

Hoover was fascinated by the potential of science as a weapon against crime. Soon after taking over, he involved the bureau in the use of fingerprinting, which had been used by law enforcement since the turn of the century. Hoover also began to hire scientists from outside the bureau as consultants on a case-by-case basis. When Goddard's laboratory began a training program, he enrolled Special Agent Charles Appel.

Appel returned from his studies and put together plans for a laboratory at the bureau. On July 7, 1932, he proposed that the bureau establish "a separate division for the handling of so-called crime prevention work . . . " that would include a "criminal research laboratory." Hoover approved and the laboratory was ready by September.

The laboratory was housed in a room within an old railway building. It contained only basic equipment, including a microscope on loan from an optical instruments company and photographic equipment. Appel managed to get a used carpet from another office and was given enough money to order some cabinets to hold supplies. Even with scant equipment and a staff of one man, the laboratory was soon a major contributor to bureau investigations. Within a year, the laboratory had handled about 1,000 examinations, mostly involving ballistics and handwriting analysis. Today, with 500 employees, the laboratory processes about a million pieces of evidence a year. The variety of evidence is almost endless. It includes pieces of clothing, paint chips, metal fragments, bullets, fibers, blood, computer files—just about anything related to crimes and crime scenes.

Appel's laboratory did not remain in its existing quarters for very long. In 1934 it was moved to the Justice Department building, where bureau headquarters was housed. The laboratory followed the FBI's move to the J. Edgar Hoover FBI Building in 1974. It remained there until April 2003, when it transferred to its own home in Quantico, Virginia, outside of Washington.

The FBI laboratory is housed in three five-story buildings at Quantico, Virginia. Costing $155 million, the laboratory has elevators reserved for carrying evidence to the laboratory spaces on the

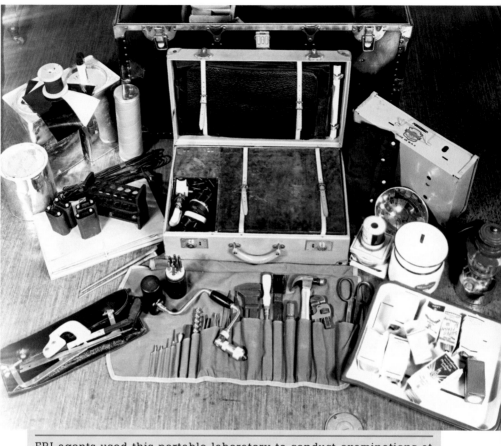

FBI agents used this portable laboratory to conduct examinations at crime scenes in the 1930s. (*Corbis*)

upper floors. Air in the laboratory sections is 100-percent sterile to combat contamination of evidence. Huge bays are located on the ground floor. These are large enough to hold the fuselage of an aircraft, if necessary.

LABORATORY MISSION

Appel's vision for the laboratory was very exact and still describes its mission today. "I believe the Bureau should be the central clearing house for all information which may be needed in the criminological work and that all police departments in the future will look to the Bureau for information of this kind as a routine thing . . . ."[2]

The state-of-the-art FBI Laboratory is located on the grounds of the FBI Academy in Quantico, Virginia. *(David Brabyn/Corbis)*

Today, the laboratory provides technical and forensic services to a wide variety of law enforcement organizations, including local and state police departments as well as other federal agencies. Usually, but not always, the cases from local and state agencies handled by the laboratory involve violent crime. Scientists from the laboratory also provide expert testimony in court. Teams of special agents trained by the laboratory regularly support law enforcement agencies in the United States and abroad in major investigations and handling disasters.

In 2007, the 75th year of forensic science service by the FBI, laboratory director Dr. Joseph A. DiZinno noted, "In the early 1920s and 1930s, law enforcement agencies, including the FBI, were only beginning to see the value of using science to solve crimes. In 1932, when the FBI moved a few pieces of laboratory equipment into room 802 of the Old Southern Railway Building in Washington, D.C., it was with the vision that the federal government could use its considerable knowledge and resources to help state and local law enforcement solve crimes and actually prevent crimes from occurring."[3]

The laboratory has more than 20 specialized units that carry out forensic investigations on-site and in the field. Some units are designed to respond to incidents or assist in the collection of evidence in the field. The Explosives Unit, for example, specializes in handling evidence related to bombs and incendiary devices. Several units focus on examining and analyzing evidence in the laboratory, including units specializing in fingerprints, handwriting, ballistics, chemistry, and DNA.

FORENSIC EVIDENCE

The finest scientific minds and technology count for nothing without evidence that has been meticulously collected and preserved. Evidence must be uncontaminated and admissible in court. The Evidence Response Team Unit works with Evidence Response Teams (ERTs) that are employed by all 56 of the bureau's offices. Their job is to gather all possible evidence from crime scenes.

ERTs made up of agents at the FBI's field offices have a reputation of being the best crime scene investigators anywhere. These teams consist of agents trained by the Evidence Response Team Unit for evidence gathering, although they usually have many other duties as well. The ERTs can be composed of a few or dozens of agents, support personnel, and event experts called in from the outside. Some field offices also have teams for unusual situations, such as underwater evidence recovery.

Some of a field office's ERT personnel are always on call to respond to significant cases under FBI jurisdiction. State and local police also may call on FBI ERTs for help. In a typical year, ERTs may respond to more than 2,500 calls. An ERT member never knows what to expect when the call goes out. ERTs were on the scene at the 9/11 attacks in New York City, Washington, D.C., and Shanksville, Pennsylvania. They were at the Alfred P. Murrah Federal Building in Oklahoma City after it was blown up by Timothy McVeigh in 1995. Sometimes ERTs are summoned for disasters dissimilar to crime or terrorism. They were on scene, for example, at the Columbia space shuttle disaster in 2003 and the Minneapolis bridge collapse in 2007. They also may be used overseas, as they were during the 2004 tsunami in Southeast Asia and the investigation of mass graves in Kosovo after the war in the former Yugoslavia.

FBI Evidence Response Team Unit members photograph evidence near a creek at Kit Carson Park in Escondido, California, as part of a search for a missing teen. *(AP Photo/Denis Poroy)*

WORKING TOGETHER

A scenario describing a shooting investigation provided by the FBI in 2008 provides an example of how agents and scientific personnel working in the field and the laboratory work together to gather and analyze evidence. The report is titled "Covering All the Angles. Our Experts Reconstruct Shooting Incidents."[4]

Police officers raid the house of a suspected drug dealer. He emerges from a doorway, holding a pistol, which he fires at an officer. The shot misses and shatters a portion of a wall. As the suspect dives into a bathroom, the officer and his two partners return fire. Four different

TRACE EVIDENCE

Forensic science pioneer Dr. Edmond Locard developed a principle that became a basic concept of law enforcement: A criminal always leaves something behind at a crime scene and carries something away when he leaves. The items involved can be bits of hair, paint chips, glass shards, grains of soil—almost anything. Usually small, these items are called "trace evidence." Because trace evidence includes so many different types of items, virtually the full array of laboratory equipment can be brought into play to study it.

Every year, 10,000 pieces of trace evidence pour into the FBI laboratory's Trace Evidence Unit. There, it is compared, analyzed, and contrasted in every way possible for whatever clues it may contain. Often, the clues are too small for the eye alone to detect.

Experts at the Trace Evidence Unit can tell if a strand of hair is dyed or has been burned, whether it is from an animal or human, where on the body it originated, and whether it has been shed or pulled out. They can determine the direction of a blow that broke a piece of glass and what kind of instrument did it. They can determine whether tiny bits of building material are insulation, fiberglass, tile, or brick. From these and other traces, cases are made.

guns are firing. Miraculously, only one person is injured, a man who had been sleeping in a back bedroom, hit by a bullet that had passed through several walls and caused only minor injuries.

After the shooting, local police call in experts from the FBI laboratory to reconstruct the incident. Their job is to understand how the shooting unfolded. Where was the shooter standing? How far away from him was the man who was hit? Painstaking care enables them to fully detail what happened. Not only do they document 198 bullet holes at the crime scene, but they also could tell with a high degree of certainty who had fired the bullets, where the shooters were positioned when they fired, and which gun fired the shot that hit the sleeper.

A reconstructed shooting or other crime scene can look like a science project. Agents first construct a grid so that the placement of every item of evidence can be recorded and measured. In the case of a shooting, once bullet holes are located, long, thin metal dowels, called "trajectory rods," are inserted into the holes. This process determines the angles taken by the bullets. Computer graphics may help the determination of angles to be even more precise. If a shooting occurs in a house, where there are many right angles, aligning measurements in a grid is easier than if it takes place outside.

Back at the FBI laboratory, scientists and technicians can microscopically compare bullets and shell casings gathered at the scene. Weapons can be test-fired into a specially designed water tank that allows a bullet to remain intact after firing. Weapons and the bullets they fire can be matched.

An investigation such as the one described above involves field agents, firearms examiners, and graphics specialists. Using old-fashioned tools such as tape measures and protractors as well as the newest laser scanners, they provide the information needed by investigators and, if the case goes to trial, prosecutors.

CODIS

No forensic technique has made more news in recent years than the use of DNA to track and convict criminals—and sometimes exonerate the innocent. The FBI laboratory's CODIS Unit is at the forefront of this area. CODIS stands for Combined *DNA Index System*. The job of the CODIS Unit is to manage and direct the system. CODIS is a system

TRAINING AT THE BODY FARM

The "Body Farm," as it is popularly called, is the University of Tennessee's Forensic Anthropology Facility. The three-acre site is really where the bodies are buried. About 50 bodies are donated to the farm annually. They are placed in environments similar to those that investigators may find at crime and accident scenes. FBI ERT agents train at the farm each May. On the second day of a typical course in 2009, agents were introduced to maggots. Dr. Ian Dadour, a forensic entomologist, held up a maggot and explained how pinpointing a maggot's age can tell a lot about what it is eating.

The maggots at the larval stage of the blowfly have helped investigators solve a host of crimes. They hatch from eggs laid by adult flies on corpses. Since entomologists know how long it takes for an egg and maggot to develop, investigators can use the maggots to determine how long a corpse has been dead.

FBI ERT members learn about the different facets of using maggots in forensics during their training at the farm. They also get their hands dirty. Duct-taping themselves into Tyvek body suits for protection, the agents spend two days practicing locating, marking, and excavating human remains, under strict evidence-recovery protocol. Even though many of them have had experience at the job before, the sights and smells are not pleasant.

One agent taking the 2009 training described the experience. "I don't think anyone could just walk in here and deal with the smell and also the sight of a human being decomposing," said Medora Arnaud, a field photographer from the Houston field office. "But you know you have a job to do. And I'm sure a lot of times that's what gets a lot of people through it."[5]

of DNA databases of more than 5 million genetic profiles of convicted criminals. These DNA profiles are maintained by a broad spectrum of crime laboratories: federal, state, and local. Beginning as a trial program in 1990 serving 14 state and local authorities, CODIS now involves 170 agencies in United States and 40 agencies in 25 foreign countries.

Basically, CODIS allows federal, state, and local forensics laboratories to electronically store, maintain, search, swap, and compare DNA profiles from crime scenes, offenders, and missing persons. DNA can come from blood or other body fluids, bones, cigarette butts, shirt collars—in short, almost anything with which a person has had contact. DNA profiles—which look like a series of numbers—from crime scenes can be matched with samples in the CODIS data already taken from criminals. DNA from different, seemingly unrelated crime scenes can be compared. Biological relatives of missing persons can supply their DNA to see if it matches that from unidentified remains. All such information can be shared by every law enforcement agency in CODIS, enabling them to pool resources.

The value of CODIS was stressed in testimony by Captain Don L. Means of the Forensic Science Division of the Washoe County (Nevada) Sheriff's Office before the Nevada State Senate Commission on the Judiciary on April 19, 2007.

According to Means, "Without the DNA database, we would never have convicted Joaquin Hill for first-degree murder in November 2006 . . . Verdi is not heavily traveled and this was one person coming through."[6]

The case he was describing was the murder of 80-year-old Alice Mosconi in the town of Verdi on June 8, 2001. She was found bludgeoned to death in a scene that veteran police described as extremely bloody. In October 2005 DNA from the woman's pantyhose was linked to a sample from convict Joaquin B. Hill, also known as Kiven Johnson. He had been serving a nine-year prison term in California for auto theft and drug charges. In October 2004 his DNA had been added to the California DNA database due to a burglary conviction.

A case cited by the North Carolina State Bureau of Investigation as a CODIS success story began when a lone male, armed with a handgun, entered the State Employees Credit Union in Raleigh, North Carolina, on August 13, 2003. He approached a teller and commanded, "Give me all your money," firing his weapon for emphasis. Two employees placed money on the counter, which the robber grabbed. As he ran from the bank into the parking lot, he again fired his weapon, this time into the ceiling. He then fled on a bicycle.

Police called to the scene found that the robber had discarded his blue shirt on the roadside as he fled. A DNA profile taken from the shirt was sent to CODIS. On searching the database, North Carolina officials found that the robber had already been caught and held by the FBI on other bank robbery charges.

When Charles Appel began his first day of work in his single-room laboratory, he could not have envisioned a time when FBI agents and scientists would track down criminals at the molecular level.

World War II

In 1921 a German named William Sebold left the country of his birth to work in aircraft factories and other industries in South America and the United States. He became a U.S. citizen in 1936. In 1939 he returned to Germany for a visit. There, he was contacted by the Nazis and asked to spy on his adopted country once he returned to America. Sebold agreed, but only after he had talked with the U.S. consulate in Cologne, on the Rhine River. Loyal to the United States rather than to the Nazis, Seblod had become a double agent. His decision would enable the FBI to break a major Nazi spy ring in the United States on the brink of the nation's entry into World War II.

CHANGING TIMES AND MISSIONS

For many Americans, the armed conflicts in Europe and Asia that preceded World War II were not a primary concern. Americans were worried about feeding and housing themselves and their families. The Great Depression, which began with the stock market crash of 1929, was in full force. Nevertheless, abroad there were wars. Imperial Japan had invaded Manchuria, then China. Fascist Italy had invaded Ethiopia, hoping to revive lost colonial ambitions in Africa. Nazi Germany had annexed Austria and grabbed parts of Czechoslovakia. The three countries signed pacts that created an alliance, called the "Axis," after the Rome-Berlin axis. When Hitler ordered German forces to invade Poland on September 1, 1939, World War II erupted.

A directive from President Franklin Roosevelt in 1939 strengthened the FBI's authority to investigate subversives within the United States. The directive was reinforced by the Smith Act, which Congress passed in 1940. The new law outlawed advocating violent overthrow of the government.[1]

The situation in which the FBI found itself on the eve of World War II is much like conditions that the bureau confronts today, although the cast of characters and enemies were different then. The FBI had just emerged from an era of conflict with violent gunslingers; John Dillinger was barely in his grave when Hitler and the Nazis came to power in Germany. The violence unleashed by Adolph Hitler would be on an infinitely more horrendous scale that the shoot-outs with Dillinger and his fellow gangsters. Still, there are parallels with the challenge facing the FBI since 9/11—a monstrous new menace from abroad had to be confronted while dealing with homegrown threats, old and new.

The FBI of today has to protect the nation against domestic terrorists. As the April 1995 bombing of the federal building in Oklahoma City demonstrated, homegrown Islamic terrorists are not the only perpetrators of domestic terrorism attacks. Moreover, terrorism by residents of the United States, and even its citizens, within its borders is not new. Just prior to and during World War II, the FBI also had to use some of its resources on home front subversives as well as agents from the Axis enemy bent on destroying democracy.

Unrest at home was spawned partly by the economic distress and uncertainty of the Great Depression. The American Communist Party, with secret backing from the Soviet Union, tried to influence organized labor. Its ultimate goal was revolution that would turn the United States into a Soviet-style state. At one point, the Communist Party of the United States and similar groups had a million members.[2]

Since the Soviets eventually sided with the United States and its allies against the common Nazi enemy, however, the FBI ultimately focused on the more immediate threat from domestic fascists. There were plenty of them—mostly sympathizers of Nazi Germany. The most notorious organization was the German-American Bund, which supported Nazi ideals and goals.

During the second half of the 1930s, the FBI was undergoing what amounted to on-the-job-training in counterintelligence. Even before the FBI set up its Special Intelligence Service in June 1940, the agency had broken some major cases. Fifty spies operating on American soil had been detected before the United States actually entered the war, according to FBI records.[3] The most astonishing and meaningful in terms of protecting the homeland was cracking the Duquesne Spy Ring, with the help of double agent William Sebold.

THE DUQUESNE RING

The Duquesne Spy Ring was a well-oiled, superbly organized group of Nazi spies headed by a veteran spy named Fritz Duquesne. Born in Cape Colony, South Africa, Duquesne lived a life so adventurous and exotic that it seems like far-out fiction. Known in Africa as the Black Panther, he was a big-game hunter, journalist, saboteur, assassin, and spy.

Duquesne was a *Boer*. The term is the Dutch word for "farmer" and is used to describe people of Dutch and French Huguenot descent, also known as Afrikaners, who settled in South Africa starting in the middle of the 17th century. Duquesne fought against the British in the Boer War of 1899. He was captured, escaped, and ended up in Britain. There, he joined the British army under an assumed name to carry on the war from within. Back in South Africa as a British officer, he spied for the Boers and engaged in sabotage. His lifelong hatred for the British and their commander Lord Kitchner was fanned by the murder of his sister by British troops and his mother's death in a British concentration camp. Caught again by the British, he was imprisoned in Bermuda. He escaped again and in 1902 immigrated to the United States, where in 1913 he became a naturalized citizen.

Handsome and known for spinning great stories, Duquesne was a charmer, a ladies' man, and a superb actor who assumed identities as different as a German scientist, an Australian cavalry commander, and a Russian duke. He covered the Russo-Japanese War for a New York City newspaper. He also managed to meet and become friendly with Theodore Roosevelt.[4] When World War I broke out, his hatred of the British caused him to volunteer as a German spy and saboteur. Under different aliases, he traveled to South America and placed bombs aboard British ships.

PHOTOGRAPH OF FREDERICK DUQUESNE
TAKEN JULY 1, 1940, BY FBI AGENTS.

PHOTOGRAPH OF FREDERICK DUQUESNE IN
EARLIER DAYS FOUND IN HIS POSSESSION
WHEN HE WAS ARRESTED JUNE 28, 1941.

FREDERICK DUQUESNE AND WILLIAM SEBOLD,
TAKEN BY FBI AGENTS MAY 29, 1940

FREDERICK DUQUESNE, TAKEN MAY 29, 1940,
BY FBI AGENTS.

Cameras in the hands of FBI agents snapped the upper left and
two lower pictures of unsuspecting Nazi master spy Frederick
Duquesne, who was arrested on June 28, 1941. Duquesne's portrait
(upper right) was found in his possession at the time of his arrest.
William Sebold *(with Duquesne in lower left picture)*, a German-
born nationalized and loyal U.S. citizen coerced into the Duquesne
spy ring by the Gestapo, kept FBI agents informed of the ring's
activities. *(AP Photo)*

In 1917 he was arrested for fraud in New York City and arrange-
ments were made to extradite him to Britain. Duquesne managed to
convince doctors he was paralyzed, was placed in a hospital, and then

escaped. By the time he was rearrested again in 1932, the statute of limitations on his fraud charges had expired and police could not hold him. He then set up various businesses in New York City.

He would soon return to spying. German intelligence recruited him for espionage within the United States. When he began his work in the United States in 1940, he was put in contact (and eventually paired) with William Sebold, who, it turned out, was as clever an impersonator as Duquesne.

Sebold had served in the German army during World War I. However, at great risk, he proved his loyalty to his adopted country. Although war clouds were sweeping over Europe, Sebold returned to Germany in 1939 to visit his mother in the town of Mulheim. No sooner had he arrived in Germany than an agent of the feared secret police, the Gestapo, approached him. He would be contacted by authorities soon, the agent said. Sebold then moved on to his mother's town to find temporary employment.

In September members of the German Secret Service visited Sebold. They questioned the naturalized American about military aircraft in the United States. Then came the inevitable request: Would Sebold be willing to spy for Germany upon his return to the United States? Sebold knew that members of his family living in Germany would be in danger if he refused.

Meanwhile, Sebold had lost his American passport. He went to the consulate in Cologne for a new one. While there, he told staff members he had been recruited as a Nazi spy. He wished, Sebold said, to cooperate with the FBI on his return. He was told to play along with the Germans, thus taking on the dangerous role of double agent.

The Nazis taught Sebold how to send coded messages by shortwave radio, to take microphotographs, and other tricks of the spy trade. They told him that on his return to the United States he would be "Harry Sawyer," a diesel engineer. They also gave him five microphotographs containing instructions on the information he was supposed to find in the United States and how to send it to Germany by code. Three of the photographs were to be given to other spies already in America.

When Sebold arrived in America, the FBI went to work. The FBI laboratory built a shortwave radio station that Sebold could pretend was his. From there, over the course of 16 months, they sent 300 false messages to Germany and received 200 from the Nazis in return. Nazi spies in New York City revealed themselves to Sebold by giving him messages to transmit to their superiors in Germany. They provided information on national defense and the departure of British ships from New York.

FBI agents helped Sebold set up a business office that they could observe. It was outfitted with a hidden microphone and a two-way mirror—state-of-the art surveillance equipment in those days. Agents hidden on the other side of the mirror in an adjacent office filmed meetings between Sebold and a parade of German agents who visited. Among them was Duquesne. He told Sebold how to start fires in industrial plants and showed him plans for a new American bomb stolen from a plant in Delaware.

All in all, FBI agents gathered information about and identified 33 German spies. Most were captured in a major raid carried out by 93 agents on the night of June 29, 1941, and a few others were rounded up shortly afterward. They went to trial and, to the shock of his handlers in Nazi Germany, the main witness was "Harry Sawyer." All were convicted or pled guilty. They were sentenced less than a month after the Japanese bombed Pearl Harbor. Duquesne, by then 65 years old, was sentenced to 18 years in prison and a fine. In Leavenworth Federal Penitentiary, Duquesne was not popular among the other inmates, who beat and mistreated him. He was released because of failing health in 1954, and he died a pauper at age 79 in a New York City hospital on Welfare Island.

Sebold, protected by authorities, faded into history. Because of him, many historians believe, the Nazi spy machinery was nipped in the bud before the United States entered the war and it never fully recovered.

WAR FOOTING

Once bombs rained down on Pearl Harbor, the FBI went on a war footing (heightening security, mobilizing military forces, and gearing up industry to increase production of military necessities). According to war plans already established, J. Edgar Hoover put the bureau on a 24-hour, seven-day-a-week schedule. The FBI Academy began to churn out agents to boost manpower. Preparations for war included the FBI's identification and listing of German, Italian, and Japanese aliens in the United States who were considered threats to security. Only a few hours after Pearl Harbor was attacked, President Roosevelt ordered the FBI to arrest these people for deportation from the country. More than 3,800 of them were taken into custody in five days.

ND-98

Sebold was the most daring double agent used by the FBI during the war, but he was not the only one. The FBI recruited many double agents, a process that enabled them to learn the inner workings of how German intelligence operated. Another man, given the code name "ND-98" by the FBI, was the owner of an import-export business. Born in Germany, he was a naturalized U.S. citizen. The FBI gave him that name after he volunteered to become a double agent, not out of patriotism but for pay.

ND-98's job was to convince the Germans that he had a secret radio station on Long Island, New York, from which he could pass on information that would help the Nazi cause. The Nazis took the bait and asked ND-98 to send them information about troop movements and industrial production of war material such as aircraft and arms. The FBI prepared plenty of information that convinced the Nazis that the information was genuine, but it had no real significance. With help from the military, the FBI also prepared messages that misdirected German troop movements. For example, ND-98 would suggest to the Germans that the Allies were preparing to attack a certain place on a certain day, luring their forces away from the real target. ND-98's telegraph key was an important weapon in the U.S. war effort. It helped win several battlefield objectives through the D-Day invasion of Normandy.

INVASION

A mini-invasion of U.S. soil began shortly after midnight on a dark, surf-lashed beach near Amagansett on Long Island, New York. Slipping through the inky night, a German submarine landed four men. They wore their military uniforms so they would be treated as prisoners of war, not spies, if caught while landing. They hauled ashore explosives, primaries, and incendiary devices for a campaign of sabotage against American war production. Four nights later, a similar group landed on a Florida beach with the same intent: to sabotage American industry and transportation and spread fear among the population.

The plot was hatched by German intelligence and put under the command of Lieutenant Walter Kappe, who had spent several years in the United States as a German-American Bund member trying to garner support among German Americans for the Nazi cause. Kappe found his candidate saboteurs among Germans who, like him, had lived in America but returned to their homeland. The dozen selected were trained in explosives, arson, codes, and how to blend into American society. Familiarization with different types of industry and transportation networks was part of their training. They were to mount a two-year campaign of terror once they landed on American shores.

A TRAGIC EPISODE

One of the most tragic episodes that occurred on the home front during World War II was the hysteria that led to the relocation of 120,000 Japanese residents of the United States—more than half of them U.S. citizens—in internment camps. Most of the Japanese and Japanese Americans imprisoned were from the West Coast states of California, Oregon, and Washington, which were considered geographically most vulnerable to attack by Japan. President Franklin Delano Roosevelt authorized the internment with Executive Order 9066 on February 19, 1942.

After the war, the action was considered a disgrace and a violation of the civil rights of the people interred. Congress apologized for the act in 1988 and financial reparations were made to the victims and their heirs.

A footnote to history is the fact that J. Edgar Hoover strongly opposed internment of the Japanese, arguing vigorously against it. Hoover asserted that the FBI already had arrested resident Japanese aliens who might prove to be a threat. The roundup was not necessary, Hoover argued, but he was ignored.

According to an FBI statement, "The purpose of the invasions was to strike a major blow for Germany through destruction of America's ability to manufacture vital equipment and supplies … to strike fear into the American civilian population and diminish the resolve of the United States … ."[5]

The four-man team that landed on Long Island was led by 39-year-old George John Dasch. With him were Ernest Peter Burger, 36; Henrich Harm Heinck, 35; and Richard Quirin, 34. The spies that entered

Edward John Kerling, alias Edward John Kelly *(left)*, and George John Dasch are two of the eight Nazi saboteurs captured by the FBI. Kerling led the group that landed at Ponteverda, Florida, and Dasch led the group that landed by submarine at Amagansett, Long Island. *(Bettman/Corbis)*

BUSINESS AS USUAL

Focus on the war did not mean that the FBI could neglect its usual business, such as combating crime and civil rights investigations, which foreshadowed the enforcement of the civil rights laws to come. Racial segregation was legal in the 1940s and was practiced even in the armed forces, with black-only units under white officers, as well throughout the defense industry. African-American groups pressured the president to appoint a Fair Employment Practices Commission (FEPC) to try to reduce segregation in industry. Although it had no enforcement power, the FEPC ordered the transit workers union in Philadelphia to end segregation within its ranks. The union refused and went on strike. The commission called in the FBI, which had the power to arrest individuals who hampered the war effort. The strike qualified as impeding defense so the FBI prepared to arrest its leaders. They backed down and the order went through.

through Florida were leader Edward John Kerling, 33; Werner Thiel, 35; Herman Otto Neubauer, 32; and Herbert Hans Haupt, 22. Dasch and Burger had both become naturalized U.S. citizens, with Dasch even serving honorably for a brief time in the U.S. Army.

Both teams buried their uniforms and equipment on the beach. Wearing civilian clothes, they started to move out. The Florida team split up, sending two men to Chicago and two to New York City. The team on Long Island barely escaped capture when a lone Coast Guardsman on patrol spotted them. Unarmed, he pretended to accept a bribe they offered to ignore them, and then reported them to his headquarters. By the time a Coast Guard squad reached the beach, they had fled to New York City.

Perhaps because of the close call, Dasch got cold feet. He called the FBI in New York, saying he had just arrived from Germany and was headed for Washington, D.C. Once there, he said, he would contact FBI headquarters. He was true to his word and was taken into custody.

Questioned by agents, Dasch revealed all. The three other members of the Long Island team were arrested in New York City on June 20. The Florida group members were nabbed in New York and Chicago a few days later. All were tried by a military court. Dasch and Burger were given prison sentences and in 1948 they were released and deported. The other spies were executed on August 8, 1942.[6]

GEARING UP FOR THE NEXT WAR

Although the Soviet Union was fighting with the Allies against the Nazis, the U.S. government knew that that alliance would not outlive the war due to the Soviet Union's own objectives. The Soviets were eager for territory and influence and were dedicated to exporting their brand of communism to the world.

In the spring of 1944 Russian troops were advancing into Germany from the east, Americans from the west. The two met on the eastern bank of the Elbe River, at what became the border between Communist East Germany and free West Germany.

Even as a classic photograph was taken of American and Russian soldiers shaking hands to celebrate victory over the Germans and mutual friendship, Soviet agents were at work in the United States. And the FBI was on their trail.

Cold War Espionage

During World War II the FBI was occupied by the threat of potential Nazi spies and saboteurs in the United States. As a result, it could not focus on the covert buildup of a Soviet espionage network that was going on within the nation's borders. Nor, for that matter, was the FBI aware of how many Soviet spies actually had worked their way into the United States. Soviet espionage was well underway in the United States even while both countries fought together against the Germans. Compared to the Soviet Union's numerous intelligence operatives and the well-oiled apparatus supporting them, the World War II spies working for Nazi Germany were amateurs and their attempts at espionage were stumbling. The Soviets infiltrated agents throughout American society and even into sensitive government positions. When World War II ended, the FBI had to shift gears quickly and cope with the new danger from the former comrade-in-arms of the United States. It was a daunting challenge.

TRAITORS AND TURNCOATS

Many Soviet and Communist sympathizers among Americans were influenced by the fact that the Soviets had stood alongside the United States in the war against fascism. Most were not themselves enemies of the United States. Rather, they simply felt that communism offered a better way of life for the masses of average people than democracy.

Once the war was over and the rivalry between the Soviets and the United States became one of competing superpowers, some of the many Americans who had sympathized with communism when the Soviet Union was an ally against the Nazis became disillusioned with Moscow. They realized that the Soviets threatened to impose a tyranny of their own and their sympathy for the Soviets faded. Some Americans who had been actively helping the Soviets even flipped to the American side.

Perhaps the most important American defector from the Soviet espionage establishment was Elizabeth Bentley. A Connecticut native, she was a brilliant woman who had been educated at Vassar College, Columbia University, and the University of Florence in Italy. An idealist, Bentley joined the Communist Party of the United States. In 1938 she began working for an Italian library in New York City that was a front for fascist propaganda. She volunteered to spy on her employer's activities for the Communists, thus beginning her espionage career. By the end of World War II, Bentley, by then an alcoholic, had a change of heart about the Soviet Union and went to the FBI. She provided significant information about the Soviet spy network with which she had worked. Beyond that, she agreed to continue her activities for the Soviets while serving as an FBI informer.

From Bentley and others like her, the FBI learned the extent of Soviet spy operations in the United States. Intelligence services in Canada and Great Britain also discovered that Soviet spies were active in their countries. Gradually, with the help of the Allies, the FBI began to track down and expose Soviet agents who had been woven into the fabric of American society and the U.S. government. The bureau had to walk a fine line. The Red Scare of the early 1950s fanned by Wisconsin Senator Joseph McCarthy and the smear tactics he used threatened to tarnish legitimate efforts to sniff out individuals who were actual Soviet threats.

Meanwhile, a small-scale attempt by the U.S. military to learn about and counter Soviet spy networks was beginning to bear fruit. In 1943 the U.S. Army had begun a project code-named VENONA. The project's aim was to intercept and break the codes of messages sent from Soviet spies in the United States to Moscow. The original aim was to intercept Soviet diplomatic messages. "American analysts quickly discovered that these Soviet communications dealt with not only diplomatic subjects but also with espionage matters."[1]

VENONA

Most of the Soviet messages were not successfully decoded by VENONA code breakers, but those that were decoded contributed immensely to uncovering Soviet espionage in the United States. The project began in February 1943 under the army's Signal Intelligence Service, a forerunner of the National Security Agency. Based in Arlington, Virginia, it was started by a young employee of the service, Miss Gene Grabel, who had been a schoolteacher only two weeks earlier.

VENONA intercepted thousands of Soviet messages—a slow and difficult job. The project monitored transmissions from several different Soviet organizations, ranging from diplomats to the KGB. In 1943 the first break in the Soviet diplomatic code was made by an army officer who had been an archaeologist in civilian life. A year later, the KGB code was penetrated but not completely deciphered. In total, about 2,200 VENONA messages were translated.[2] It was enough, though, for VENONA to help crack major Soviet spy efforts, the Rosenberg ring, and others as well.

ATOMIC SPIES

VENONA, as well as information and court testimony from Elizabeth Bentley, was critical in the FBI's outing of a ring of spies that did more damage to the United States and the free world in general than any other. Run by American citizen Julius Rosenberg—Soviet code-name "Liberal"—it stole secrets from the United States that helped the Soviet Union build its first atom bomb. Rosenberg and his wife Ethel were committed members of the Communist Party and ardent supporters of the Soviet cause. He was a natural for the spy business because he worked for the U.S. War Department (later Department of Defense) until the war's end. VENONA analysis of messages sent to Moscow during the war revealed that Julius transmitted significant amounts of sensitive information on military technology such as radar and missile guidance systems. It also disclosed that as early as 1944, someone had been sending Soviet intelligence the names of scientists working on the

Julius Rosenberg and his wife Ethel stand during their espionage trial in New York in March 1951. *(AP Photo)*

Manhattan Project, which developed the atomic bomb. That person was at first identified as "Liberal" and later as Rosenberg.

The FBI had been gathering evidence on the Rosenberg ring before September 23, 1949, when President Harry S. Truman announced, "We have evidence that within recent weeks an atomic explosion has occurred in the U.S.S.R."

FBI agents were already in Los Alamos National Laboratory in New Mexico and other sites at which the atomic bomb had been developed. They began to interview and question scientists, seeking clues to the identity of the atomic spies. The trail led to a British scientist, Klaus Fuchs, a Communist who had worked at Los Alamos. After British authorities arrested him in February 1950, at American request, he admitted involvement. Fuchs had passed his information through an American he knew as "Raymond" (Philadelphia chemist Harry Gold). The FBI tracked him down, and he confessed to working under instructions from the former Soviet vice-consul in New York City. Gold said the information he passed on came from army man David Greenglass, who had been assigned to Los Alamos in 1944 and 1945.

The FBI pounced on Greenglass. He led agents to the ring's leader, Julius Rosenberg. His wife, Ethel, also involved in the ring, was Greenglass's sister. He admitted passing the Rosenbergs classified information, including sketches of an atomic bomb. Others were also implicated. Communist Max Elitcher, an ordinance engineer working for the U.S. Navy, led the FBI to Morton Sobell, a radar engineer who also gathered information for the Rosenbergs. Elitcher, it turned out, had refused Rosenberg's efforts to recruit him.

The extent of the Rosenbergs' penetration of the U.S. defense effort is illustrated by an astonishing fact that Greenglass revealed to agents: The Rosenbergs knew that he was working on the atom bomb before he did. Greenglass had been stationed at Los Alamos for three months when his wife, Ruth, came to visit him. She told him that Julius, at dinner in New York City, had mentioned that her husband was involved in the bomb project. Greenglass was surprised, perhaps even shocked. He had no idea that the research in which he was involved was part of a larger effort to develop a nuclear weapon. That disclosure was not the end of their conversation. Ruth said that Julius and Ethel had asked for Greenglass to provide information on the bomb research. Their argument was that Russia was an ally and had a right to the information that the United States had tried to hide from it.

After hedging, Greenglass began to supply the Rosenbergs with information on the research underway at Los Alamos. Harry Gold also served as a go-between. He visited Greenglass in New Mexico and identified himself with part of a cardboard Jell-O box. (Earlier, Julius had provided David and Ruth with a piece of a Jell-O box, saying their contact would have another piece, which would match.)

FBI agents arrested Greenglass in June 1950 and the Rosenbergs the following month. The others were soon taken into custody. The subsequent trial of the Rosenbergs was one of the most sensational in U.S. history. On March 29, 1951, they were found guilty, on April 5 sentenced to death, and on June 19, 1953, executed at Sing Sing Prison, Ossining, New York, a few minutes apart. The executions came after a massive campaign of protests, pressure on the White House, and legal appeals by Communists and their sympathizers and people opposed to the death penalty. It continues to be a controversial event in American history.

ENEMIES ON THE INSIDE

No covert operative is more dangerous than a "mole," a spy who spies on spies. In the jargon of the espionage world, a mole is a spy who becomes part of and works from within the ranks of an enemy governmental staff or intelligence agency. The 1980s saw a string of arrests of moles by the FBI, not all of them working for the Soviets. John Anthony Walker Jr., a U.S. Navy warrant officer and communications specialist, was sentenced to life in prison for sending the Soviets secrets compromising a million code messages. Ronald William Pelton, a communications specialist with the highly secret National Security Agency, became another lifer due to giving the Soviets details of U.S. information collection programs. Jonathan Jay Pollard, a civilian intelligence analyst for the navy, was sentenced to life for spying for an American ally—Israel. Sharon Marie Scranage, a CIA clerk in Ghana, went to prison for five years for providing that country details on CIA operations there. CIA intelligence officer Larry Wu-tai Chin committed suicide before he was sentenced for providing inside information to China. Dozens more spies were caught by the FBI during the 1980s.

During the 1990s, the FBI was particularly concerned with the possibility that moles had burrowed into America's intelligence community, particularly the Central Intelligence Agency. Between 1992 and 2001, the FBI devoted huge resources to finding Russian spies and was highly productive and made several arrests. Especially significant was the arrest in February 1994 of Aldrich Hazen Ames, a veteran CIA case officer, and his wife, Rosario. Ames specialized in the Soviet foreign intelligence service, Komitet Gosudarstvennoy Bezopasnosti (KGB). His job was to get Russian spies to turn their loyalties. Instead, it was Ames who, aided by his wife, turned for more than $1 million in payment. Ames passed on information about CIA and FBI covert operatives and operations against the Russians. The FBI eventually homed in on Ames and conducted a 10-month surveillance operation. He was caught and sentenced to life imprisonment, his wife to 63 months.

Although the Ames case was over, the FBI had indications that there was another mole buried deep in American intelligence, one particularly difficult to dig out. The suspicion was correct, but the details were not. The FBI sought a mole in the CIA and eventually focused on one CIA employee. He was temporarily suspended from duty while the FBI prepared a case against him. Before he could be prosecuted, however, the FBI realized it had pinpointed the wrong suspect in the wrong agency. The mole was one of the FBI's own.

His name was Robert Hanssen, an FBI agent and counterintelligence expert with 25 years of service to his credit. Most of that time, it turned out, he had spied for the Russians, first for the KGB, then for its successor, the Russian Federation's Sluzhba Vneshney Razvedki (SVR). His work in FBI counterintelligence placed him in a position from which he had easy access to sensitive information.

Known to fellow agents as something of a maverick, Hanssen was the son of a Chicago policeman who joined the FBI in 1976 at age 32. Before that, he had been an accountant and a Chicago police officer. He was known as a devoted father and husband and, along with his wife and six children, he attended church regularly. Hanssen also was involved in Opus Dei, a conservative and controversial Roman Catholic lay organization that espouses a highly spiritual approach to life. Hanssen had problems getting along with his coworkers, but his personal life seemed spotless. He had no problems with drugs or alcohol, voiced anticommunist views, and lived quietly.

Hanssen first contacted the Soviets in 1979. The details of his spying career are outlined in a review of the FBI's performance in the case carried on by the Department of Justice, Office of the Inspector General (OIG).[3] His espionage spanned three separate time periods: 1979–1981, 1985–1991, and 1999–2001. The 674-page report stated: "Hanssen compromised some of the nation's most important counterintelligence and military secrets, including the identities of dozens of human sources, at least three of whom were executed." Two of the executed were KGB officials based in Washington who were working as double agents for the Americans. When they returned to Moscow, they were tried and sentenced to death.

The more than 20 packages that Hanssen provided the Soviets contained thousands of pages of classified documents and computer disks containing U.S. plans in the event of nuclear war, major developments in military weapons technology, and details of active spy cases. Hanssen earned about $600,000 in cash and diamonds for his treason. He was also promised $800,000 more that would be in a Moscow bank account.

Hanssen was arrested in Vienna, Virginia, where he and his family lived, in February 2001. Agents apprehended him after he parked his Ford Taurus in a woodsy park about a mile from his home and secretly placed a package containing secret information for his Russian handlers at a prearranged drop site under a rustic wooden footbridge.

On May 10, 2002, Hanssen was sentenced in federal court to life imprisonment for selling highly classified national security information to the Russians—during and after the cold war. He was sent to the Federal Bureau of Prisons Administrative Maximum prison in Colorado, held in total isolation within a concrete cell, and allowed no contact with the outside world. He remains imprisoned today.

After his arrest, he told the FBI his espionage was for profit, but there may have been other motives, according to the OIG report. Since boyhood he had been fascinated by Kim Philby, a storied British intelligence agent who worked for the Soviets and later fled to Russia, where he died in 1988. He also was fascinated with James Bond movies and equipment used in espionage, such as a shortwave radio. The report suggested that personality factors such as low self-esteem had been a factor. It noted that as a child Hanssen had been emotionally abused by his father.

The discovery of Hanssen's treason was a huge humiliation for the FBI. In the long run, however, it had some positive results. Then-FBI Director Louis J. Freeh appointed former FBI and CIA Director Judge William Webster to head a special commission to review what went wrong in the Hanssen case. The commission recommended sweeping

FBI agents remove evidence from the home of turncoat FBI Agent Robert Philip Hanssen in February 2001. He was arrested after dropping off a package of classified information for Russian agents. *(Getty Images)*

security improvement in FBI policies and procedures, which were put into effect and have enhanced FBI effectiveness in the war on terror that began about the time Hanssen was exposed.

The Webster report, as the commission's recommendation was dubbed, called the "ease with which he [Hanssen] was able to steal" secrets "shocking."[4] Sometimes, he would carefully gather it for months. Other times, the report stated, Hanssen would "grab the first thing he could lay his hands on."

The OIG report and the Webster Commission report pinpointed many problems with FBI operations and policies that they concluded enabled Hanssen to be so successful. They included lack of a solid internal security apparatus, poor supervision, easy access to secret informa-

MISSED OPPORTUNITIES AND HIDDEN CLUES

According to the Justice Department report on the Hanssen case, clues to Hanssen's hidden life went unnoticed and opportunities to detect his espionage were missed. Hanssen's personality flaws, such as desire to demonstrate superiority and his lifelong fascination with spying, went unnoticed. He once hacked into sensitive information with authorization for computer access but reported it to his bosses as a problem with the office's computers. He had a physical altercation with a female employee for which he received a five-day suspension. At times he acted arrogant, aloof, and sour toward fellow agents.

The FBI's focus on the CIA rather than its own house was partly due to the fact that the CIA was not an equal partner in the investigation, says the OIG report. Hanssen also knew how to evade identification; even his Russian handlers never met him in person. At some point late in 2000, the spotlight fell on Hanssen. Although the FBI has never confirmed the details, Hanssen's involvement was revealed by a contact within Rus-

tion, and failure to follow up on signs that Hanssen might have been a rogue agent. Most telling was a finding of the Webster Commission that focused on FBI culture itself. Until the attacks of September 11, 2001, and despite cracking many spy cases, the commission noted, the FBI's system remained geared toward detecting and prosecuting traditional crime. Its internal culture was based on cooperation and free exchange of information within the bureau. It was, said the report, "a work ethic wholly at odds" with the restricted, need-to-know sharing of information in intelligence work.[5]

The FBI acted to correct these problems. Among the improvements were the creation of a security section, better monitoring of the finances of employees, and more polygraph tests for people with access to high-security matters. However, by the time the analysis sian ranks. The FBI has described how it was given a bag of evidence containing documents, computer disks, and a tape recording. Hanssen's thumbprint was on the wrapping. Analysis of the tapes revealed his voice and handwriting on a note was also his. Hanssen was placed in a job at FBI headquarters where he could be watched. His office, car, and computer were secretly searched. When he went to make a drop-off, he was arrested. He talked openly about sensitive information to people who had no "need to know." He seemed to spend money more lavishly than he normally might on an agent's salary. Hanssen's brother-in-law, an FBI agent as well, reported to his superiors in 1990 that Hanssen had thousands of dollars of cash hidden in his home, but the bureau did not follow up on the lead. The report also says that Hanssen's wife discovered him reviewing a communication from the Soviets in the basement of their home but he talked his way out of it. After his arrest, he told FBI agents he had confessed his treachery to an Opus Dei priest after his wife's discovery. Whether or not this is true is not known.[6]

of what went wrong with the Hanssen disaster was conducted, a far greater national catastrophe had occurred. In the aftermath of 9/11, the FBI's entire intelligence program came under scrutiny, and a major overhaul was needed to cope with the new challenge of 21st-century terrorism.

Organized Crime

Apalachin, New York, is a small town near the city of Binghamton on the Susquehanna River. It has a claim to fame that its residents—a few more than 1,000 people as of the 2000 census—probably would like to forget. One chilly day in the middle of November 1957, a soft drink bottler named Joseph Barbara had a barbeque outside the 11-room stone house on his 53-acre estate. Several of those in attendance had stayed overnight at a local motel. They presented themselves as businessmen in the soft drink industry who were there for a meeting. They were there for a meeting, all right, but not about soft drinks. On the meeting's agenda were drug trafficking, territorial disputes in New York City, and other activities of Italian-American organized crime.

Barbara was more than a soft drink bottler. He was a lieutenant in Buffalo's Italian-American mob, a ranking member of the American Mafia (or Cosa Nostra, Italian-American organized crime). The meeting at his estate included more than 100 mobsters, not only from the United States but from Canada and Italy as well.

Local and state police had long suspected Barbara of criminal connections. When Sergeant Edgar Croswell, a New York State trooper, heard a meeting of his associates was to occur on the estate, he decided to investigate. He brought along another trooper and two agents of the U.S. Treasury Department.

They found more than 30 large luxury cars parked in the estate's driveway and a crowd of men gathered in the yard near a smoking barbeque pit. When the troopers started to jot down license plate numbers of the cars, the members of the party saw their uniforms and scattered. Some jumped into cars while others hightailed it into the woods.

Croswell had the road blocked and soon 62 of the guests were detained by police for questioning before they were released. Never before had law enforcement been able to question so many big names of organized crime at one time. Among them were Joseph Bonanno, Carlo Gambino, Vito Genovese, and Joseph Proface. When the FBI checked the names taken by officers against its files, 40 had criminal records.

Former mobster Joseph Valachi testifies before a Senate subcommittee. Valachi's testimony, coupled with the bust of the meeting in Apalachin, New York, confirmed the existence of interconnected groups of criminals, or families, across the country. *(Bettmann/Corbis)*

The curiosity of Sergeant Croswell triggered a revelation that made headlines across the nation. For the first time, law enforcement had hard evidence that big-time crime was truly organized; that regional bosses of the various mobs conspired and consulted with one another; in short, that the Mafia was firmly established in the United States. After Apalachin, there was no doubt that a nationwide alliance of criminals, sometimes linked by blood and always by mutual interests, was running major crime enterprises throughout the country. Apalachin was living, physical proof of testimony before the U.S. Senate Special Committee to Investigate Crime in Interstate Commerce in 1950 and 1951. Witnesses described to the committee, chaired by Tennessee Senator Carey Estes Kefauver, the existence of a secret Mafia in the United States—the first

A BLIND EYE?

What the FBI did before Apalachin about organized crime—specifically Italian-American organized crime—is a matter of controversy. Critics of J. Edgar Hoover, particularly, say he turned a blind eye toward the Mafia or even denied its existence. Others say that Hoover's focus on violent crime and Communist subversion put organized crime at a much lower priority level.

The FBI has long been sensitive about such allegations and attempts to refute them for all to see. As early as 1946, the FBI stresses, it started a General Investigative Intelligence Program to develop information on criminal activities, including organized crime's involvement in bookmaking and other rackets. By the early 1950s, it had gathered "considerable information" on racketeers throughout the country. In 1953 field offices were asked to gather information on top mobsters in their areas. However, many racketeering activities, such as gambling and loan sharking, were beyond the FBI's reach. Federal law did not give the bureau jurisdiction over these activities.[3]

The campaign against organized crime started to grow muscles in 1961 when Attorney General Robert Kennedy created an time many Americans outside the Italian-American community had heard of it.

The FBI defines a criminal enterprise as a group of individuals with an identified hierarchy, or similar structure of ranking among its members, engaged in significant criminal activity.[2] Organized crime, according to the FBI definition, is any group with a formal structure whose main objective is to make money through illegal activities.[3] Both definitions fit the gathering at Apalachin.

In 1963 Italian-American organized crime suffered another blow at the hands of Joseph Valachi, a Mafia "soldier," the lowest rank of Mafiosi, who can serve in roles as varied as driver and hit man. Valachi was the first member of the Mafia to break *omerta*, the code of silence.

Organized Crime and Racketeering Section in the Department of Justice. Its job was to coordinate activities by the FBI and other agencies in the department against the mob. As Congress realized the magnitude of the Mafia threat, it passed laws giving the FBI greater jurisdiction over crimes such as gambling and authorized the use of court-approved electronic surveillance (wiretaps) in cases involving organized crime.

The most important law in the FBI's arsenal for combating organized crime is the Racketeer Influenced and Corrupt Organizations Act (RICO) of 1970. It enables the FBI to target an entire organization rather than individuals suspected of an assortment of crimes. RICO gives the FBI broad powers over 35 different crimes, including eight state crimes, such as murder, in special cases. RICO has been used in many areas besides organized crime, and can be employed against any business that commits more than one type of racketeering. Equally important has been FBI expertise in long-term undercover penetration of the mob and encouraging mobsters to turn against their counterparts. During the 1980s, more than 1,000 Mafia mobsters were convicted of various crimes. However, their ranks were refilled.

Never before had a member of the Mafia publicly acknowledged its existence. He spilled all he knew—and made up more—about the Mafia in the United States and Italy. Valachi also revealed an insider's name for the Mafia, one now used routinely by the FBI: *Cosa Nostra,* meaning "Our Thing" or "This thing of ours."

The Apalachin meeting and Valachi's testimony fully exposed the invisible empire of the Mafia by demonstrating the existence of interconnected regional groups that coordinated their criminal activities. After Apalachin, organized crime became a priority for the bureau during the second half of the 20th century and remains so today.

The Mafia is no longer the only major organized crime organization in the United States. Other ethnic "Mafias," as they are sometimes called, have become well established. They include the following:

- Russian mobsters who fled to the United States after the Soviet Union collapsed
- African crime organizations from countries such as Nigeria involved in drugs and financial scams
- Asian crime rings, including Chinese tongs and the Japanese Yakuza
- Criminal organizations based in Eastern European nations such as Hungary and Romania[4]

These groups compete, but they also cooperate, or at least hesitate to infringe on one another's turf. Moreover, they utilize modern technology such as the Internet, which is often used in Nigerian identity theft and investment scams.

The FBI estimates that the illegal profits of global organized crime total about $1 trillion a year. Money comes from subtle activities such as manipulating the stock market and such outwardly brutal operations as human trafficking. To combat this vast network, the FBI has three units in its Organized Crime Section:

- Cosa Nostra, Italian organized crime, and racketeering
- Eurasian/Middle Eastern organized crime
- Asian and African criminal enterprises

SICILIAN VESPERS

The origins of the name *Mafia* are mysterious. In Sicily the term has come to be connected with the concept of men who are due respect. One of the most colorful and long-lasting stories about the origin of the term dates to the 13th century. It is linked to a historical event, an uprising that has come to be known as Sicilian Vespers.[5] Then, as has often been the case in history, the Sicilians were under the heel of foreign oppressors. In this case it was the French Angevin Dynasty, which ruled Naples as well.

The uprising began in Palermo at the time of evening prayers, called "vespers." There are several explanations of what triggered it. Both involved French soldiers. In one version, soldiers checking people for weapons began to molest Sicilian women. In another, a French solider who had had too much to drink made aggressive advances upon a young wife, whereupon her husband stabbed him to death. Whatever happened, mobs of Sicilians began attacking French troops, and then French people in general. The rampage spread, and for six weeks French men, women, and children were massacred.

The uprising triggered a wider war. The Angevins and the French crown, together with the papacy, were pitted against the Sicilians and Aragon, in Spain. The war and uprising spread to the Italian mainland. In the end, the Angevins lost Sicily to the royal family of Aragon.

Where does the Mafia come in? According to the story, the word *Mafia* is taken from the first letters of the words that compose the battle cry supposedly used by the rebels: *Morte alla Francia Italia anela.* It means "Death to the French is Italy's Cry."

Whether or not the story is true—and many scholars consider it a myth—the Mafia was born of traditional Sicilian resistance to authority, especially government or the rich, who were likely to be foreigners.

In a typical year, these units may be involved in more than a thousand investigations and arrests.

THE MAFIA

The Mafia has roots extending deep into the past when Sicilians and other Italians formed secret societies to resist invaders. The FBI acknowledges several different Italian criminal organizations. Four are based in Italy. The Sicilian Mafia is based in Sicily, but it is international in scope and closely linked to its American counterpart. The Camorra is based in Naples. 'Ndrangheta, in Calabria at the foot of the Italian boot (as seen when looking at a map), is known for its extreme violence and rapid rise to power in recent years. Sacra Corona Unita, an offshoot of the Camorra, is headquartered in Puglia, the heel of the boot. Except for the Sicilian Mafia, these groups have only a small presence in the United States.

In the United States the American Mafia or Cosa Nostra is, according to the FBI, "the foremost criminal threat to American society." Cosa Nostra in America, says the FBI, is separate from the Sicilian Mafia but both groups cooperate. It is composed of groups called "families," each with its own geographic operating area. Among the illegal activities the FBI ascribes to Cosa Nostra are murder, extortion, drug trafficking, corruption of public officials, gambling, loan sharking, money laundering, labor racketeering, prostitution, stock manipulation, and infiltration of legitimate businesses. Labor racketeering—profiting by control of unions—is historically one of the crimes most important to the mob.

The Mafia in America developed out of gangs of Italian immigrants in cities such as New York and New Orleans during the late 1800s and early 1900s. Among the most notorious of these gangs was the "Black Hand," *Mano Nera* in Italian. It specialized in extortion and sometimes kidnapping for ransom. A favorite tactic was to send relatives of victims the ear of their loved one to spur them into providing ransom money. During the 1920s, gangs grew into large organizations within big cities, such as the Chicago mob run by Al Capone, whose parents came from Naples. The roots of Cosa Nostra, however, were strongest in New York City, where it was solidified by gangsters Joseph Masseria and Charles "Lucky" Luciano. To organize the various criminal groups, Luciano set up the system of families headed by bosses, or *dons*, to use the Sicilian term. According to his scheme, a commission of bosses settled disputes between families, a system that has not always worked.

In recent years the FBI has focused on the Gambino organized crime family, one of five major families in New York City. In 2009 the acting boss of the family, John D'Amico (alias Jackie "the Nose") was charged with the 1989 murder of Frederick Weiss, believed to be a government informant. The FBI did not have to go far to find him. D'Amico was already in custody. He was one of 62 mobsters, including the leadership of the Gambino family, rounded up by the FBI and other law enforcement agencies in February 2008. The charges involved murder, extortion, and racketeering going back to 1976. They involved attempts to control the construction industry and its unions. Also grabbed were mobsters associated with the Genovese and Bonanno families. The Gambino family, however, suffered most because the raids wiped out its top ranks.

The family had already been reduced to a shadow of its former self by relentless FBI investigation. It led to the downfall of John Gotti, the notorious and powerful head of the family from the middle of the 1980s to the early 1990s. Gotti was known as the slippery Teflon Don, because he repeatedly was acquitted of serious charges, mainly though intimidating witnesses and jury tampering. He was an iconic mob leader, a flashy dresser who gave lavish neighborhood parties. He came to power by having rival Paul Castellano gunned down at a New York City steakhouse in 1985.

The FBI and New York City Police pursued Gotti tenaciously, using electronic surveillance and old-fashioned detective work. Their break came when Gotti henchman Sammy "The Bull" Gravano betrayed his boss by cooperating with police. Gotti was convicted on 13 counts, including the murder of Castellano, in 1992. He died in prison in June 2002.

THE NEW "MAFIAS"

The news media have been reporting on the Gambino family for years. Today, however, the names associated with the new "ethnic Mafias," as they are sometimes called, are far from Italian. Instead, they are names such as Vyacheslav Ivankov, the Solntsevo organization, the Young Joon Yang gang, and the Yakuza. Criminal groups and individuals within the United States that operate here but are closely tied to those in other lands have become an FBI focus. These groups often do not confine their activities to the United States. Some report to bosses in their native countries.

Eastern criminal groups are linked to countries in the Baltics, the Balkans, Central and Eastern Europe, Russia, the Caucasus, and Central Asia. Some of the Asian groups are traditional, even ancient. These include the Chinese triads and tongs and the Japanese Yakuza.

Some of the ethnic Mafia cases cracked by the FBI have netted big names. The first major Eurasian organized crime case in the United States took place in 1993 with the targeting of Vyacheslav Ivankov, a major Russian crime figure. He had a reputation for extorting money from individuals who he threatened with torture and death. In Russian, the equivalent of a Mafia don is called a "thief-in-law." Ivankov was a thief-in-law who headed a syndicate operating in Moscow, Budapest, London, Vienna, Toronto, and New York City. During testimony before Congress in 1996, then-FBI Director Louis J. Freeh called him "one of the most powerful Russian crime leaders in the country."[6] He arrived in the United States to coordinate activities for Eurasian-led crime in the United States. He specialized in extorting Russian businessmen and their interests.

FBI agents determined that his victims included Russian executives in a New York City firm called Summit International. The firm advised Russian immigrants on investments. Ivankov and five of his henchmen were arrested for attempting to extort the executives and then convicted. In 2004 Ivankov was deported to Russia. He apparently became involved in disputes with other crime figures there. In July 2009 he was ambushed and shot. He died from his injuries three months later.

In May 2000 an investigation resulted in the jailing of the former prime minister of the Ukraine, Pavel Lazarenko. He arrived in the United States in February 1999 and was indicted by a federal grand jury the following year. An investigation by the FBI and Internal Revenue Service over six years showed that he had extorted more than $40 million from Ukrainian citizens and had laundered more than $20

Vyacheslav Ivankov *(center)*, a top boss of the Russian mob in Brooklyn, is flanked by FBI agents while being led from the bureau's New York headquarters in June 1995. Ivankov was convicted in July 1996 of trying to extort $3.5 million from two owners of Summit International, an investment advisory firm for Russian émigrés. He was murdered in 2009. *(AP Photo/Monika Graff)*

million of it through American banks, a crime in this country. He was sentenced to nine years in prison and a $10 million fine.

Asian criminal enterprises are not new in the United States. Chinese gangs called "tongs" have been operating in Chinese communities within American cities for at least a century. They have now been joined by gangs from Japan, Korea, Indochina, the Philippines, and South Pacific island nations. A recent and new trend among these groups is cooperation across ethnic lines. Trafficking in humans for labor and prostitution is among their specialties, and they often mask or combine their illegal activities with legal businesses.

A massive investigation of human trafficking was launched by the FBI in San Francisco in 2003. Its target was individuals and businesses that were bringing South Korean women into the United States for prostitution and moving them across state lines for that purpose. In June 2005 the FBI, in cooperation with other federal agencies and San Francisco police, hit 40 locations between San Francisco and Los Angeles. Scores of illegal aliens were apprehended and 26 people involved in the ring were convicted of various crimes.

FIGHTING CRIME BEFORE IT REACHES AMERICA

The FBI works closely with foreign law enforcement agencies in the campaign against international organized crime. Its Legal Attaché Offices are an important part of this function. "Legats," as the FBI calls them, have been operating for more than 60 years. There are offices in 75 cities around the world, providing coverage in more than 200 countries. The offices are created under agreements with host nations and located in U.S. embassies and consulates. Recent operations by Legats included coordinating the FBI's role at the 2008 Summer Olympic Games in Beijing and working with the government of Georgia on the investigation into the attempted assassination of President George W. Bush during a speech in that country in 2005. Housed in the former barracks of the Royal Hungarian Mounted Police in the center of Budapest is another FBI facility geared to fight international crime as well as terrorism. It is the International Law Enforcement Academy, run in cooperation with the Hungarian government. There, law enforcement officials from across Eastern Europe and Asia have been trained. The program, lasting eight weeks, includes courses in ethics, leadership, and battling public corruption. Programs such as this are an attempt to thwart international organized crime before it is exported to the United States.

Desperados, Killers, and Kidnappers

On the last day of 2007, the FBI announced that it had renewed its focus on one of the world's most famous cold cases (crimes or accidents that have not been solved and are not the subject of current criminal investigation or civil litigation), the mystery of D.B. Cooper. In November 1971 a man calling himself Dan Cooper parachuted from a hijacked airliner into the 200-mile-an-hour wind and rain of a stormy night over the Pacific Northwest. With him went $200,000 in $20 bills, ransom he had extracted for the plane's safety. Dan Cooper— the name D.B. was given to the hijacker by the press by mistake—was never seen again. Some of the money, a rotting package containing $5,800 in $20 bills, was found on a sandbar in the Columbia River in 1980 by an eight-year-old boy. In March 2009 the FBI issued another press release describing its progress on the case and asking the public for help in the search for Cooper, something it has done for several years.

The Cooper case typifies the immense variety of violent crimes covered by the FBI. Unlike organized crime, many of these crimes are not committed by complex criminal enterprises but by individuals or loosely organized gangs. The FBI becomes involved when the crime is specifically assigned to it, such as bank robbery, or comes under its jurisdiction for other reasons, as when a fugitive or killer crosses state lines.

THE COOPER CASE

The Cooper case is an example of FBI persistence. Even though the bureau suspects Cooper was killed in his jump, it continues the investigation. The objective is to find Cooper if he is alive and, if not, discover what happened to him. The story begins on the afternoon of November 24, 1971. A man probably in his mid-40s wearing a business suit, tie, and trench coat, the so-called Dan Cooper, purchased a one-way ticket on a flight to Seattle, Washington, at the Northwest Airlines counter in Portland, Oregon. He was between five feet ten inches to six feet in height, with brown hair. Waiting for the aircraft to take off, he ordered a bourbon whiskey and soda. Once in the air, he handed the flight attendant a note and opened a briefcase. Inside the briefcase was a mass of wires and sticks, which appeared to be explosives. He had hijacked the plane for ransom. On landing in Seattle, Cooper exchanged the 36 passengers for the $200,000 and parachutes. He ordered the plane flown toward Mexico. Between Seattle and Reno, Nevada, Cooper astonished the flight crew by jumping out the rear of the plane and vanishing in the night with a parachute, an emergency chute, and the money. In 1980 an eight-year-old boy found the ransom money, badly decomposed, on a family outing on the north shore of the Columbia River in Oregon, but there was still no sign of Cooper.

The FBI was called in to investigate the case while the hijacked plane was still in the air. Agents have run down thousands of leads and questioned hundreds of suspects without success. The FBI revealed that it had a DNA sample of Cooper's from a tie he had left behind on the airplane. The case has fascinated people and is the subject of Internet forums. From the forums, an agent assigned to the case in 2007 discovered that a comic book published in French at the time of the hijacking features an adventurous test pilot and shows him parachuting. His name: Dan Cooper.

"Dan Cooper is very much alive—on the pages of a French comic book series that was popular when the hijacking occurred," says an FBI press release in 2009 asking the public to jog their memories and come up with information on the case.[1]

Possibly, the FBI suspects, the hijacker took his name from that comic book. If so, he probably saw it overseas. This theory ties in with a new FBI theory that "Cooper" was a veteran of the U.S. Air Force at some point stationed in Europe. He may have worked unloading cargo from planes by parachute. Perhaps he worked in Seattle's aircraft industry and lost his job during the economic downturn of 1970–1971. He knew about parachutes, but not enough to realize his emergency chute was a training item and sewn shut.

The search goes on for Cooper. By publicizing the case, the FBI hopes to perhaps nudge the memory of someone who knew a man fitting Cooper's description who one day in the 1970s just disappeared.

FBI agent Ralph Himmelsbach *(second from right)* asks questions of Mr. and Mrs. Harold Dwayne Ingram *(left)* at FBI offices, where it was announced that the Ingram's son Brian had found the D.B. Cooper hijacking money while on a family outing. Listening is William Wren *(right)*, who flew the hijacked plane. *(Bettmann/ Corbis)*

THE DEATH OF THE DESPERADOS

Cooper may go down as one of the FBI's most famous fugitives. No criminal ever sought by the FBI, however, can compare with the notorious John Dillinger. The death of Dillinger under a hail of FBI bullets put the bureau in the public limelight as never before. Dillinger had embarrassed the FBI at Little Bohemia, the resort in Wisconsin where agents badly bungled a raid on Dillinger and his gang. He made the FBI's reputation when agents shot him dead outside the Biograph Theater in Chicago, which was showing a gangster movie starring Clark Gable.

Dillinger was a one-man crime wave. He robbed banks. He attacked police stations to get weapons. He and his men murdered people who stood in their way. He was also as elusive as smoke, escaping jails and ambushes. In the words of the official FBI description of the history of the Dillinger case, "… he and his violent gang terrorized the Midwest, killing 10 men, wounding seven others, robbing banks and police arsenals, and staging three jail breaks—killing a sheriff during one and wounding three guards in another."[2] Like the "Teflon Don" John Gotti of New York City's Mafia, he seemed out of reach of law enforcement, as again and again he escaped dragnets. Dillinger was betrayed by Anna Sage, a friend of his girlfriend, Polly Hamilton. An illegal alien, she hoped to avoid deportation and also wanted the $5,000 reward. She got the reward but was returned to her native Romania. Wearing an orange skirt to alert agents, Sage accompanied Dillinger and Hamilton to the movies.

Seeing the trio, the agent in charge lit a cigar, the signal for agents and police officers to close in. The experienced Dillinger sensed their presence and ran toward an alley while reaching for his .380 Colt semi-automatic pistol. Agents opened fire and he fell dead. After frustrations and embarrassments, the FBI had its man.

The FBI and partnering law enforcement agencies also tracked down Dillinger's gang. Among them, Lester Gillis, known as Baby Face Nelson, died in a shootout with FBI agents, Harry Tommy Carroll was shot by police, and Harry Pierpont was captured and executed.

RADICALS

The rebellious and tumultuous era of the 1960s—including civil rights struggles, counterculture movements, and protests against the Vietnam

War—spawned radical gangs that in the 1970s turned to extreme violence. These gangs, in a sense, had a foot in the past and another in the future. On one hand, they acted like desperados of old, robbing banks and shooting it out with police. On the other, they were very much terrorists, but homegrown rather than foreign. None was more violent and notorious than the Symbionese Liberation Army (SLA).

The SLA was the focus of what the FBI calls "one of the strangest cases" in its history, the kidnapping of heiress Patty Hearst.[3] The case began at about 9 P.M. on February 4, 1974. Hearst, a college student and the 19-year-old granddaughter of newspaper magnate William Randolph Hearst and daughter of millionaire George Hearst, was in her apartment in Berkeley with her fiancé, Steven Weed. Someone knocked on the door and in burst a gang of men and women, guns drawn. They beat up Weed, grabbed Hearst, tossed her in the trunk of their car, and drove away.

The kidnappers were radicals that called themselves the Symbionese Liberation Army. (The name was taken from the word *symbiosis*, denoting different organisms working together.) SLA members were black and white, men and women. Basically, they were anarchists and extremists trying to incite guerilla war against the U.S. government, but they claimed they were trying to liberate blacks. The group was led by hardened criminal and escaped convict Donald DeFreeze. By the time of the kidnapping, they had shot two school officials in Oakland, California, with cyanide-tipped bullets, killing one.

They kidnapped Hearst because her family was famous and powerful. The crime fulfilled two aims: striking at the establishment and grabbing pubic attention. The SLA demanded that the family provide millions of dollars in food donations as ransom. Meanwhile, they kept Hearst locked in a closet, abusing her and brainwashing her into joining their cause.

Two months after the kidnapping, the nation was stunned by an audiotape with Hearst saying she was joining the SLA's fight against oppression. Less than two weeks later, she was photographed holding an assault weapon during a bank robbery, covering her fellow SLA members.

The FBI, working with other law enforcement agencies, launched a massive search for Hearst and the SLA. It was a difficult job because the terrorists had frightened witnesses, operated through safe houses, and had excellent security. In the end, however, they caught themselves. Two of the group tried to steal items from a Los Angeles sporting goods store but fled when a guard resisted. Their getaway van was discovered and led authorities to the safe house where the gang was hiding. The SLA was surrounded by law enforcement officers and a full-fledged gun battle, lasting two hours, began. The house caught fire and DeFreeze and six of his followers died.

Hearst was not among them. She and others had escaped and fled. The FBI stayed on her trail as she and the remnants of the SLA moved

CRUISE SHIP CRIME

About 10 million Americans a year travel on ships traversing international waters, most of them holiday cruise ships. During the course of a year, the FBI may investigate several cruise ship crimes—32 in 2005. The majority of crimes on cruise ships are assaults, both sexual and physical. Missing persons cases are rare, despite the high-profile press coverage they receive when they do occur. Death investigations by the FBI occur mostly on commercial vessels.

The FBI becomes involved under several circumstances, including the following:

★ If the ship is U.S. owned, whatever the nationality of the victim or suspect
★ If the crime occurs within 12 miles of the nation's coast, which constitutes territorial waters
★ If the victim or perpetrator is a U.S. citizen on a ship that departed from or is arriving at a U.S. port
★ If the crime is an act of terrorism against the United States

Outside of U.S. authority, FBI legal attaches work with local police on investigations involving U.S. citizens. Sometimes foreign law enforcement authorities invite FBI experts to take a major role in an investigation.[4]

around the country. She was finally captured in San Francisco on September 18, 1975. Charged with bank robbery and other crimes, Hearst went to trial. She claimed that she had been brainwashed into joining the SLA's cause, but the jury found her guilty. After serving two years of a seven-year sentence, her sentence was commuted by President Jimmy Carter. President Bill Clinton later pardoned her. She married, raised a family, and has worked as an actress.

As far as the public was concerned, the SLA and the Hearst case faded into history; but this was not the case for the FBI. One by one, agents tracked the remaining SLA members down. The last of them was arrested in South Africa in 2002 and extradited to the United States. Only then did the FBI close the case.

The robberies committed by the SLA to finance their activities demonstrate how terrorism is often linked to bank robberies and other crimes. At times, it can be difficult to distinguish between terrorists who commit other criminal acts and run-of-the-mill criminals. Law enforcement officials fear alliances between the two, just as they warn that drug and human smuggling rings could as easily sneak terrorists across the nation's borders as their usual merchandise.

GANG VIOLENCE

If anything, the street gangs of today are even more violent that the radicalized gangs of the 1970s. They also tend to be larger and more organized. Some, such as large outlaw biker gangs, even verge on and cooperate with organized crime. Others are in cahoots with large foreign drug cartels, especially those in Mexico. The FBI is the principal federal agency with jurisdiction to address violent street gangs. It uses its Safe Streets initiative with other law enforcement agencies. The FBI also has developed National Violent Crime, Drug and Gang Strategies that serve as a framework for combating violence. The FBI's Safe Streets and Gang Unit administers 152 Violent Gang Safe Street Task Forces. Like other task forces, these groups consist of officers and agents from other law enforcement agencies as well as FBI agents.

The FBI attacks drug trafficking and gangs by focusing investigations on entire criminal enterprises rather than individuals. It looks at all of the facets of a criminal operation—money laundering, for

BANK ROBBERY

The FBI has been chasing bank robbers since the days of John Dillinger. Although bank robberies sometimes are overshadowed in the public's eye by terrorism, drugs, and violent street crime, they still occur regularly. Sometimes they are as violent as the worst street crime. In May 2007, for example, a robber fatally shot two bank employees in Bessemer, Alabama, before he was shot and captured by police who happened to be driving by the bank. The FBI says that because of its focus on terrorism, it is depending more on local and state police to help with bank robberies. In a typical year, more than a thousand banks may be robbed within the United States. FBI figures for 2008, for instance, give the total number of banks hit by robbers as 1,617.

instance—and goes after them all. By using sophisticated wiretapping and other advanced technological tools, agents go after the entire gang, from street level thugs and dealers up through the command structure to gang leaders. The FBI's approach differs from that of the Drug Enforcement Administration (DEA), whose mission is entirely the enforcement of drug laws. Operating under laws such as RICO, the FBI can target crimes committed by drug rings not directly considered drug trafficking in itself, providing a one-two punch with the DEA.

An example of how the FBI uses RICO to attack gangs resulted in the July 2009 conviction in Las Vegas, Nevada, of five members of the Aryan Warriors, a white supremacist gang that, like the better-known Aryan Brotherhood, began in prison and migrated to the streets. The gang is extremely violent and has a reputation for threatening prosecutors in cases against its members. The charges involved a host of crimes, including murder, extortion, illegal gambling, identity theft, and fraud.

The July 2009 convictions were for conspiracy to engage in a racketeering organization (RICO) or conspiracy to distribute the drug methamphetamine. Evidence described the murder of a prison inmate, assaults in and out of prison, a stabbing, and the operation of the largest secret methamphetamine laboratories ever discovered in Nevada.

Two days before the Aryan Warriors' convictions and in the neighboring state of California, the U.S. Justice Department announced the nation's largest ever gang investigation and prosecution. Hours before the announcement, a law enforcement task force composed of 1,400 federal, state, and local officers, including the FBI, made a huge roundup of gangs across four Southern California counties as part of what was called "Operation Knock Out." The operation focused on a Latino gang in the Los Angeles suburb of Hawaiian Gardens but also hit almost a dozen others. The investigation resulted in federal and state charges against more than 200 defendants. It all began with the fatal shooting of a Los Angeles County sheriff's deputy and attacks on African Americans by the Varrio Hawaiian Gardens gang. RICO indictments involved not only the murder but also a host of other crimes, including carjackings, kidnappings, and drug trafficking.

The Justice Department deploys an array of agencies against the illegal drug trade. According to information released by the department in April 2009, efforts to combat Mexican drug cartels have been beefed up in a combination of agencies, including the DEA, the ATF, and the FBI. The bureau has created a Southwest Intelligence Group (SWIG) to assess and confront the threat to public safety on both sides of the Mexican border posed by drug cartels. SWIG now serves as a clearinghouse for all FBI activities involving Mexico. FBI drug task forces in eight Southwestern cities made thousands of arrests during 2008, according to the department statement.

CRIMES AGAINST CHILDREN

Missing children are defined by the 1982 Missing Children Act as any person younger than 18 whose whereabouts are unknown to his or her legal custodian.[5]

Since its early days tracking kidnappers, the FBI has been heavily involved in fighting crimes against children. Often, the bureau works closely with local and state police in such cases. A highly publicized case involved bringing to justice the abductor and murderer of 11-year-old Carlie Brucia in 2004. The case received widespread notoriety because a surveillance camera located at the car wash in Sarasota, Florida, where the abduction occurred caught the crime on tape.

The crime occurred on February 1. Two days later, tips led agents to arrest Joseph P. Smith. He was held on violation of probation charges. The girl's body was found February 5 behind a church three miles from the car wash. She wore only a few items of clothing. Marks on her neck

CRIMINAL PROFILING

Criminal profiling is one of the most popular FBI-oriented themes for television shows. This technique of applying psychology to violent criminal behavior was started by the FBI in 1972, when the FBI Academy launched a Behavioral Science Unit to seek patterns in the behavior of serial rapists and killers. By the 1980s, techniques had become highly effective. The National Center for the Analysis of Violent Crime was founded at the academy. It provides law enforcement with research into crimes ranging from school shootings to serial arson. Since the use of profiling began, FBI experts have helped bring down some of the nation's most notorious criminals, such as Wayne Williams, who preyed on children in Atlanta during the 1980s.

The FBI credits the Williams case with bringing criminal profiling to the forefront in serial killer investigations. The Williams investigation was in response to the killing of more than two dozen black men and boys between 1979 and 1981. Profilers determined that since the neighborhood in which the victims lived was largely African American, the killer probably was, too. Patterns emerged, including the dumping of victims' bodies in the Chattahoochee River. A stakeout was set up on the river and William was observed near where a body had been dumped at about the same time. He was ultimately convicted. The Washington, D.C., snipers, John Allen Muhammad and Lee Boyd Malvo, who terrorized the nation's capitol with random shootings in 2002, were also tracked down largely because of profiling.

indicated that she was strangled. The next morning Smith was charged with kidnapping and murder.

Agents worked to build their case against Smith. One item of evidence was a coded letter written by Smith to his brother. It was sent to decoding experts at the Cryptanalysis and Racketeering Records Unit of the FBI's crime laboratory. Smith had replaced letters of the alphabet with one- or two-character combinations of numbers and symbols, written from right to left, from the bottom of the page up. The experts cracked his code and found references to moving the body and hiding evidence. The laboratory also examined more than 100 other pieces of evidence, including DNA samples. It was enough to convict Smith of abduction and murder.

It was too late to save Carlie Brucia, but the FBI rescues large numbers of abducted and lost children. Its Child Abduction Rapid Deployment teams, designed to quickly put experienced investigators into the field, consist of four to six agents each. All together, the nationwide team consists of 48 members organized into 10 teams. They provide on-the-ground assistance to state and local law enforcement. The FBI also carries out sweeps, or major roundups of criminals engaged in a particular area of crime, such as Operation Cross Country III, a three-day national enforcement action with police departments across the country that took place in February 2009 in 28 cities. It led to the recovery of 48 children who had been prostituted. More than 500 people involved in trafficking of the youngsters were arrested.

"We may not be able to return their [the children's] innocence," said FBI Director Robert S. Mueller III in announcing the sweep, "but we can remove them from this cycle of abuse and violence."[6]

The sweep was part of the Innocence Lost National Initiative. In 2003 the FBI's Criminal Investigative Division, working with the Child Exploitation-Obscenity Section of the Department of Justice and the National Center for Missing & Exploited Children, formed the initiative to combat child prostitution. It coordinates training and action by all levels of law enforcement. By 2009, it had recovered 670 children and was responsible for many convictions of criminals involved, with some sentenced to life imprisonment.

Crime in
High Places

If FBI agents were feeling vindicated on August 5, 2009, it is difficult to blame them. After hearing evidence for more than a month in a federal court at Alexandria, Virginia, a jury convicted former Congressman William J. Jefferson, a Louisiana Democrat, on 11 of 16 charges in a bribery, racketeering, and money laundering case. In November 2009 Jefferson was sentenced to 13 years in prison. He was freed on bail while his attorneys appealed both the conviction and sentence.

During the investigation of the case, FBI agents raided Jefferson's Capitol Hill office and seized documents. Agents also found $90,000 in cash stashed between frozen hamburgers and piecrust in his home freezer. The cash came from a Virginia businesswoman who was looking for help arranging business deals in West Africa, according to the prosecution. The raid on Jefferson's office sparked harsh criticism of the FBI by some members of Congress, who accused agents of exceeding their authority and acting outside of constitutional limits.

Jefferson was charged in June 2009 with using his office to help arrange telecommunications deals in Nigeria and Ghana, oil concessions in Equatorial Guinea, and other ventures in nations throughout the region. He was accused of seeking hundreds of thousands of dollars in bribes. Ironically, Jefferson was not found guilty of the charge linked to the money in the freezer.

"The FBI has made combating public corruption its top criminal investigative priority because American citizens deserve honest and

Reporters follow former Congressman William Jefferson (D-LA) as he walks with his wife while arriving at U.S. District Court for his sentencing hearing on November 12, 2009, in Alexandria, Virginia. *(Bettmann/Corbis)*

ethical public officials," Assistant Director Kenneth W. Kaiser of the FBI Criminal Investigative Division said about the case. "He ... used his official position and office as a RICO enterprise to corruptly solicit bribes."[1]

TWIN EVILS

Over the years, FBI investigations of corrupt public officials have produced cases that have rocked the nation, and economic or white-collar crime has always been a concern. Often, these twin evils go hand in hand. The FBI has gone after crooks in business suits as actively as they have drug dealers wearing gang colors. Just as the first decade of the 21st century has seen the FBI step up its antiterror operations, the bureau has been pushed into more intense policing of financial wrongdoing such as the Enron scandal and the potential financial fraud exposed in the wake of the 2008 recession.

FBI Director Robert S. Mueller III explained the new emphasis when testifying before the House Judiciary Committee in May 2009. "Public corruption is our top criminal priority," said Mueller. As of 2009, the FBI had about 2,500 public corruption investigations under-way, with 600 agents involved.[2] In the two years prior to Mueller's testimony, 1,618 federal, state, and local officials were convicted as a result of FBI investigations.

ABSCAM

One of the most sensational—and controversial—investigations into public corruption ever carried out by the FBI was an undercover sting operation code named ABSCAM. The name came from a fake company set up by the FBI. It was supposedly run by a wealthy Arab sheik who wanted to invest oil money in valuable artworks. The company's name was Abdul Enterprises, thus the code name ABSCAM.

ART CRIME

Sometimes forgotten among cases involving corruption of high officials and violent deeds of gangs and gangsters, art theft is of major concern to the FBI. The bureau, in fact, has an art theft team of 13 agents dedicated to combating this category of crime. Art theft includes outright theft, looting, faking originals, and transporting illegal art across state and international lines. The FBI estimates losses as high as $6 billion annually.

The art theft team is supported by three special trial attorneys and maintains a National Stolen Art File, a computerized index of reported stolen art and culturally important items for use by law enforcement agencies anywhere in the world. One of the key areas pursued in recent years is the looting and theft of stolen archaeological artifacts from museums and sites in Iraq during conflict there.

Posing as representatives of the sheik, FBI agents started out after mobsters and ended up arresting members of Congress. They turned up evidence that exposed wide-ranging public corruption as well as an art theft ring. The targets included mobsters trying to hock stolen paintings and elected officials peddling influence in Washington, D.C.

The probe began in July 1978, when agents embarked on a campaign to catch New York City underworld figures that were dealing in stolen art and fraudulent stocks. After Abdul Enterprises was established, the FBI found an informer who connected undercover agents to mobsters marketing stolen paintings. Within a few months, the agents had recovered two paintings worth a total of $1 million. The agents did not stop there. In the course of the investigation, they met criminals who were dealing in fake stocks and bonds. They were able to prevent the sale of $600 million in fraudulent securities.

When they cast their net for art thieves, the agents had not expected that the haul would also include corrupt politicians. Their criminal contacts led them to politicians in Camden, New Jersey, who offered to arrange for a state gambling license in Atlantic City—in exchange for a bribe. The agents decided to see how far they could take their sting. The sheik who employed them, they told the politicians, wanted asylum in the United States. The politicians set up a meeting with U.S. congressmen who could put through legislation to get the sheik into the United States. It would cost $50,000 up front and the same amount later.

In the end, four members of Congress and one U.S. senator were arrested and found guilty on bribery and conspiracy charges, as were several New Jersey state and local politicians. Questions were raised about entrapment of suspects, but were overruled.

WATERGATE

Of all the public corruption investigations that the FBI has undertaken, the most notorious by far was the scandal that started with the June 17, 1972, burglary at Democratic National Committee headquarters in the Watergate apartment complex, Washington, D.C. Other investigations have reached as high as Congress, but this one went higher, to the president of the United States, Richard M. Nixon. The FBI was investigating its ultimate boss.

The story is familiar. Police nabbed five Watergate burglars, and then found bugging equipment and lookouts across the street from the scene of the crime. It was just the beginning of a scandal that shook the nation to its core. The campaign to re-elect Nixon had been caught in an illegal political dirty trick but, when confronted, his administration had tried to cover it up. It took two years for the scandal to reach a boiling point—the resignation of the president to avoid almost certain impeachment.

The FBI was called in as soon as the implications of the burglary were evident. Almost from the beginning, the bureau was caught in a crunch; no investigation had ever been as politically sensitive. To make matters worse, J. Edgar Hoover had died only five weeks before and FBI headquarters was in a state of unease.

Not unexpectedly, the White House pressured the FBI to bury the case. L. Patrick Gray, who was acting director due to Hoover's death, was accused of caving in to the pressure and resigned on April 27, 1973. While the probe continued under new director Clarence Kelly, "Deep Throat," the code name the whistleblower who tipped off *Washington Post* reporter Bob Woodward to the Watergate story, identified in 2005 as FBI Deputy Director Mark Felt, continued to leak information about the scandal.

Despite the turmoil, agents persisted in the investigation. They had help from the special prosecutor's office created by the U.S. attorney general and the Senate Select Committee on Presidential Campaign Activities. The probe was so widespread that almost every field office was involved. Agents prepared masses of reports and conducted 2,600 interviews for the special prosecutor. History records the downfall of Nixon and his administration and the conviction and jailing of many of his aides and operatives.

CROOKS IN EXECUTIVE SUITES

"Apart from public corruption, economic crime remains one of our primary concerns," Mueller also told Congress. White-collar crime involves acts aimed at profiting from illegal business deals, avoiding payment or loss of money, and using illegal means to give a business an advantage.

White-collar crimes investigated by the FBI include money launder-ing, security and commodities fraud, bank fraud and embezzlement, health fraud, defrauding the government, and certain environmental crimes. White-collar crime that attracts FBI attention is usually highly organized and large enough to be regional, national, or international in scope. The types of health care fraud that the FBI targets include those that involve the entire system, such as large-scale false billing schemes. Fraud in financial institutions involving $100,000 or more also brings in the FBI. The FBI will generally become involved in telemarketing or insurance fraud that is national or international in scope.

The FBI has partners in fighting financial crime. These include the federal Securities and Exchange Commission, the Internal Revenue Service, the U.S. Postal Inspection Service, the Commodity Futures Trading Commission, and the Department of the Treasury's Financial Crimes Enforcement Network.

SIGNS OF THE TIMES

In his 2009 testimony Mueller noted that the FBI's mortgage fraud caseload has more than tripled in three years, from more than 800 cases to more than 2,400. Additionally, 560 corporate fraud investigations were underway, including several directly related to the financial crisis of 2007–2009. The FBI has had to increase the number of agents investigating mortgage fraud from 120 to more than 260 since the recession. Crooked individuals preying on homeowners who feared losing their homes and making hay out of a wild mortgage market during the recession were having a field day. One way to judge the increase in such crimes is by the rise in Suspicious Activity Reports (SARs), documents that can be filed with the government by financial institutions that suspect wrongdoing. Mortgage fraud SARs increased more than 36 percent to 63,173 during (fiscal year) 2008. The estimated amount of money that could be involved is in the billions. The FBI beefed up its operations, using computer technology, undercover operatives, and wiretaps to investigate companies that engaged in suspicious property transfers. A National Mortgage Fraud Team was established in 2008 at FBI headquarters. Its job is to assist FBI field offices in the investigation of mortgage fraud, to identify the worst offenders, and to assign priority to key investigations. The FBI also has a role in 42 mortgage fraud task forces scattered across the county and participates in a Mortgage Fraud Working Group, under the Department of Justice.[3]

Mortgage fraud uses several tactics to fund, purchase, or insure mortgage loans, including misrepresentation and deception. Among the variety of mortgage fraud scams are lending fraud and foreclosure rescue scams. Lending fraud often involves falsely inflating a borrower's income or property values, thereby "qualifying" them for loans that they should not receive, which leads to missed payments and possible foreclosure down the road. Foreclosure scams are carried out by criminals who prey on homeowners in danger of losing their homes, taking fees for falsely promising to prevent it. These two types of fraud were among those involved in the takedown of 406 defendants during Operation Malicious Mortgage in 2008.

The operation was a concerted effort carried out with several other law enforcement agencies to disrupt individuals and organizations engaged in mortgage fraud. The arrests, part of 144 cases, were made between March 1 and June 18. The FBI estimated that $1 billion in losses were caused by the schemes involved in these cases.[4]

Another issue of the times, health care, also figures prominently in FBI investigations. The FBI, in fact, is the main federal investigative agency combating health care fraud. Federal and state governments finance almost half of the about $2 trillion in annual health care costs. About $60 billion of the costs are lost to fraud. Working with other federal agencies as well as insurers, the FBI can have more than 2,000 open health care fraud cases a year. In 2008 alone, bureau investigations led to 700 health care fraud convictions.[5]

ENRON: CORPORATE GREED

The beginning of the 21st century was marked by some of the highest-profile financial crimes ever cracked by the FBI. The cases involved people who were at the top levels of the corporate world. Their important positions, however, did not provide them any immunity from the reach of the law.

No case did more to awaken the public to corporate misdeeds than the investigation of the huge energy company Enron Corporation. The case was the largest and most complex white-collar investigation in FBI history. Enron officers engaged in deceptive accounting practices, including lying about earnings, falsifying cash flow, and concealing debt, that misled investors about its financial condition. Investment banks and other business partners helped Enron continue the lie by falsifying financial books.

The Enron story began in December 2001 when the company, believed to be financially robust, declared bankruptcy. When it went down, it took with it the life savings, college plans, health insurance, retirement plans, and livelihoods of thousands of its employees and stockholders. Immediately, the FBI field office in Houston, where Enron headquarters were located, assigned two agents to investigate. Agents and support staffers quickly grew to 45. Many agents were brought in from other field offices because of their expertise in ferreting out complex corporate maneuverings. Eventually, the investigation involved a task force composed of agents, analysts, and federal prosecutors based in Houston and Washington, D.C. Their job was to follow paper trails and examine complex accounting documents and the flow of money. Their goal was to find out how Enron officials managed to perpetrate fraud on such an immense scale and to provide the evidence to convict those responsible.

The effort to convict crooks in high corporate positions was as intensive as any FBI investigations of spies and gangsters. In January 2002 agents searched Enron's 50-story corporate headquarters building for nine days. They dug out critical documents and other evidence that filled 500 boxes. Over 100 interviews provided new leads to be followed. Agents eventually conducted more than 1,800 interviews in the United States and abroad.

In February 2002 Enron's board of directors issued findings from its own internal investigations. It said that Enron executives gained millions of dollars by violating the basic principles of accounting. Agents also extracted evidence from computers, obtaining corporate e-mails and a vast amount of other data, opening up still more leads. Financial analysts combed through hundreds of bank and stockbroker accounts for fraudulent purchases and illegal stock trading.

The investigation found that Enron's real operations were hidden behind a smokescreen of schemes and that its supposed financial good health was a mirage. A company that once boasted annual revenues of more than $150 billion, Enron ripped off the state of California, selling energy to its financially desperate utilities at overinflated rates. When the Internet bubble was expanding, the company overstated its new

THE ORIGINAL PONZI SCHEME

The Ponzi scheme is named after Charles Ponzi, an Italian immigrant who lived in Boston, Massachusetts, at the beginning of the 20th century. Ponzi, who was eventually deported and died in 1949 in Brazil, was a highly successful swindler. He made millions on the type of scam that now bears his name. Ponzi schemes take advantage of the desire of people to "get rich quick." The FBI warned in 2009 that Ponzi schemes are especially common during tough economic times.

Ponzi guaranteed investors a 50 percent return on their investments in postal coupons. These coupons could be exchanged for stamps. Ponzi's method of making a profit was to buy them cheaply in foreign countries and then exchange them for higher priced stamps in the United States. The problem was that he never followed through. Instead of buying coupons with the funds from the original investors, Ponzi kept the money, then convinced more people to invest. He paid the first investors with funds from the second, and so on with subsequent investors. Ponzi schemes are revealed when the operator flees or when he cannot get enough new investors to pay previous clients.

venture into broadband, causing its stock to rise without any real basis. It overvalued the worth of international properties and falsified quarterly earning reports.

Several Enron officials were convicted or pled guilty. Former Chief Executive Officer Jeffrey Skilling was sentenced to 24 years and four months in prison. Former Chief Financial Officer Andrew Fastow received a six-year term. Former Chairman and Chief Executive Officer Kenneth Lay was convicted but died before sentencing. Lay, a former U.S. undersecretary of the interior, suffered a fatal heart attack while vacationing in Colorado. At the request of his lawyers—and objections of prosecutors—Lay's conviction was abated, which is the same as though he had never been charged, tried, and convicted.

BERNARD MADOFF: THE BIGGEST SWINDLE

The fact that criminals in executive suites can destroy lives was brought home in the case of financier Bernard Madoff, who engineered what the *Wall Street Journal* called "the biggest financial swindle in history."[6] On

A *New York Daily News* front page covers the Ponzi scheme perpetrated by Bernard Madoff, who received a 150-year prison sentence for his crimes. *(NY Daily News via Getty Images)*

June 29, 2009, a judge in Manhattan federal court sentenced Madoff, 71, to 150 years in jail. Madoff also forfeited all of his property, including luxury boats and multimillion dollar homes totaling more than $170 million. He was arrested by FBI agents after a complex investigation. His sentence was the most severe ever for white-collar crime.

Madoff pled guilty to a host of charges, including investment adviser fraud, mail fraud, and money laundering. In short, he carried out an elaborate Ponzi scheme that caused losses to investors of at least $50 billion dollars. Madoff, former chairman of the NASDAQ stock exchange, had a reputation for earning unusually high profits for people who invested through him. Rather than managing their money, however, he deposited it in bank accounts, and then paid off early investors with funds received from those who engaged him later. His victims ranged from the rich and famous, such as Steven Spielberg and the co-owners of the New York Mets, to major banks and charities, to ordinary people whose life savings were wiped out.

In sentencing Madoff, Federal Judge Denny Chin described his crimes as "extraordinarily evil" and said his deeds were "not merely a bloodless crime that takes place on paper but one that takes a staggering human toll."

Protecting Civil Rights

It was not a good time for two black teenagers to be hitchhiking home from college on lonely Mississippi back roads. The year 1964 was in the middle of a decade of struggle for African-American civil rights. It was a time of the Freedom Riders, of protests, and of violence perpetrated upon both black and white Americans by groups such as the Ku Klux Klan (KKK). Henry Hezekiah Dee and Charles Eddie Moore lost their lives as a result of that violence. For 40 years it appeared that their killings by the White Knights of the Ku Klux Klan would go unsolved. However, in July 2005, the FBI and Mississippi police, responding to a brand-new federal law, reopened and solved the case.

THE RIGHTS ENFORCER

The FBI is the lone federal agency responsible for investigating charges of federal civil rights violations. It is a substantial mandate. The job entails investigation of hate crimes, both by individuals and groups, as well as racial and religious discrimination. It covers abuses and misconduct by law enforcement officials, including police brutality and evidence falsification.

Four subdivisions are included in the FBI's Civil Rights Program. The Hate Crime subprogram investigates attacks motivated by bias. The Color of Law investigates abuses by public officials, including excessive use of force by police. Human Trafficking looks into crimes involving the buying and selling of people who are forced to work in jobs such as

and prostitution. Freedom of Access addresses interference with repro-
ductive health (abortion) services.

The FBI's efforts to ensure civil rights for all goes back to its earliest
days. It battled the Klan as early as the 1920s. For many years, however, the narrow scope of laws weakened the FBI's efforts. Lynching,
for example, was not a federal crime. In the segregated South, local
authorities and juries had their own versions of justice when it came to
African Americans. In many cases, the FBI was powerless. The FBI had
no jurisdiction, for example, when in Birmingham in 1963, Alabama
Police Commissioner "Bull" Connor, a KKK member, set police dogs on
peaceful civil rights protestors. Starting in the 1960s, laws such as the
Civil Rights Act of 1964 and Voting Rights Act of 1965 greatly enlarged
the FBI's jurisdiction over civil rights crimes.

The 1964 law especially put real teeth into FBI civil rights enforcement. It banned segregation in a vast number of areas, including
schools, public places, government, and the workplace. It also made
several civil rights violations federal offenses. For example, the act
outlawed discriminatory practices that could be used selectively to bar
people from voting, in particular literacy tests for voter eligibility, which
had been widely used against African Americans.

Both the 1964 and 1965 laws were passed on a wave of public out-
rage over killings of civil rights workers by the KKK. Klansmen murdered three young activists taking part in what rights workers called
"Freedom Summer," an effort to register blacks to vote in Mississippi.
Local law enforcement, moreover, was in on the crime. The name the
FBI gave to the case—MIBURN for "Mississippi Burning"—came from
the burned remains of a station wagon used by the victims.[1]

The three activists—Michael Schwerner, James Chaney, and Andrew
Goodman—were arrested for speeding by the Neshoba County Sheriff's
office and jailed in Philadelphia, Mississippi. The Klan was told when
they were released and followed them. The FBI launched a massive
search and, tipped by an informant, found their bodies buried below
an earthen dam.

After an investigation, more than a dozen suspects, including the
county sheriff and a deputy, were arrested and charged. It took until
1967 for seven of the suspects to be convicted, but they were convicted
for conspiring to violate the civil rights of the murder victims, not for

The burned-out station wagon of three murdered civil rights workers—Michael Schwerner, Andrew Goodman, and James Chaney—was found in a swampy area near Philadelphia, Mississippi. *(AP Photo)*

murder charges. The sheriff went free. Even those sentenced received no more than six years. Among the other suspects who went free was Baptist minister Edgar Ray Killen. A lone juror later said she could not agree to find him guilty because she could not convict a preacher.

An indication of violence directed toward African Americans who tried to vote in that part of Mississippi comes from a handwritten FBI report on the MIBURN investigation in 1964. It describes a conversation between an unknown male and the wife of a jailer about a black man who had been disqualified from voting because of prior felony convictions and was being held. The man asks the wife if "the red-headed nigger could be released at eleven o'clock." When the jailer's wife said it was not possible, the man answers, "It doesn't matter, we'll get him anyway."[2]

Over the years, the media and activists kept the case in the public eye; the 1988 major motion picture *Mississippi Burning* is an example of this. In 2005, with the racial climate in Mississippi changed, a Neshoba County grand jury indicted Killen on three charges of murder. In the

The Neshoba County sheriff leads Edgar Ray Killen out of the courtroom after his arraignment in January 2005. Forty-one years after the murder of civil rights workers Michael Schwerner, Andrew Goodman, and James Chaney, Killen was sentenced to 60 years in prison. *(Landall Kyle Carter/Reuters/Corbis)*

end, at age 80, he was sentenced to 60 years in prison on manslaughter convictions. The verdict came on June 21, the 41st anniversary of the murders.

DEE AND MOORE RECEIVE JUSTICE

New developments in forensic sciences and investigative tools have improved the ability of law enforcement to solve cold cases. In 2005 Congress passed bills authorizing the Department of Justice to establish an Unsolved Crimes Section in its Civil Rights Division. In response, the FBI's Civil Rights Unit in February 2006 launched the Cold Case Initiative. The bureau has partnered in this effort with civil rights groups, including the National Association for the Advancement of Colored People, the National Urban League, and the Southern Poverty Law Center.

More than 100 unsolved murder cases from the civil rights era are under review through the initiative, according to an FBI appeal for people who have any information related to old cases to come forward.[3] In February 2009 the FBI released the names of victims of unsolved civil rights murders that occurred before 1969 in hopes that people will come forward with information on the cases.

As a result of the new law and the initiative, the Henry Dee and Eddie Moore case was revived as a hate crime investigation in 2005 after a documentary filmmaker resurrected interest in the murders. FBI agents met with Mississippi state authorities and reopened the investigation. Seeking insights from the past, agents who had worked on the original case in 1964 were asked to contribute their ideas and any relevant information.

Dee and Moore were both only 19 years of age when killed. Klansmen abducted the pair near Meadville, Mississippi. The abductors pretended to be law enforcement officers and tricked the pair into entering a car. According to Department of Justice records, the KKK suspected Dee might know about African Americans who were bringing firearms into the county. The teenagers were taken deep into the woods of Homochitto National Forest. There, the Klansmen tied them to trees, beat them badly, and interrogated them at gunpoint. Then the kidnappers bound the hands and mouths of the two with duct tape. They put their victims in the trunk of a car, drove across the Louisiana border then back into Mississippi to Parker's Landing, on a backwater of the Mississippi River. They tied Dee to an engine block and Moore to pieces of railroad track rails and threw them, still living, into the water. Their bodies were found by divers months later.

After an FBI investigation, agents and Mississippi Highway Patrol officers arrested James Ford Seale and Charles Marcus Edwards for the murders. The case was then turned over to the local authorities. At the request of the local district attorney, a justice of the peace dismissed the charges two months later.

Over the years, Seale's family claimed he had died, but the FBI found that he was still very much alive when it reopened the probe in 2005. Agents managed to convince Edwards to testify against Seale in return for immunity. Seale was charged with conspiracy and kidnapping and convicted by a jury in 2007. He received three life sentences, which he appealed but lost in June 2009.

VIOLENCE MAKES VIOLENCE

Attacks on blacks and civil rights workers by militant segregation-ists and groups such as the KKK spawned radical violence in return. Some groups of rights activists and black power organizations such as the Black Panthers turned to armed resistance. Radicals on the left and on the right committed subversive and criminal acts to further their causes. A leftist group called the Weather Underground, for example, sparked a riot in October 1969 during which hundreds of activists, wearing football helmets for protection against police, trashed a major shopping district. The group committed other acts of terror, including a bombing of the U.S. Capitol building. On the right, the KKK and other white supremacist groups tortured and killed civil rights activists. In some cases, police brutality aggravated the situation and contributed to hostility toward law enforcement among African Americans even when there was no basis for it. Throughout the 1960s into the 1970s, riots rocked inner cities across the country.

Meanwhile, growing opposition to the war in Vietnam entered the mix. Many civil rights leaders, including Dr. Martin Luther King Jr., embraced the antiwar cause. Add to this brew the rise of the counter-culture movement and spreading use of drugs, and a highly volatile situation resulted across the country. During the first nine months of 1967 alone, more than 100 people died in riots that hit more than 60 cities. Three thousand bombings by fringe groups took place nation-wide in 1970.[4] Left-wing radicals hit the Pentagon and U.S. Capitol with explosives. National Guardsmen fired on student protesters at Kent State University in Ohio, killing four. On top of all this were the assassinations of President John F. Kennedy, his brother, Senator Robert Kennedy, and Martin Luther King Jr.

DECADE OF THE ASSASSINS

No other decade in U.S. history has witnessed more assassinations of major public figures than the 1960s. The death toll is etched in the nation's memory: President John F. Kennedy in 1963, Dr. Martin Luther King in 1968, and two months later, Senator Robert Kennedy.

As far as the FBI is concerned, the cases are closed for the present. Despite so many stories to the contrary, the FBI assures that no evidence exists of conspiracies in any of the killings. The bureau conducted 25,000 interviews in the John F. Kennedy investigation. Agents followed up tens of thousands of leads. The FBI concluded that Lee Harvey Oswald acted alone and the Warren Commission, set up to study the assassination, agreed. Known racist James Earl Ray's fingerprints were found by the FBI on a rifle near the King crime scene and in a car seen there. He bought a rifle in Alabama and rented a room in Memphis near the room where King was shot. Although he later took back his confession, the FBI concludes he was the killer. Sirhan Sirhan's own lawyers did not deny that he shot Robert Kennedy. He pled insanity and the jury convicted him. In 1992 a grand jury in Los Angeles refused to reopen the case.

GOING BY THE RULES

In the middle of it all was the FBI, investigating the right, the left, and often the in-between. It was a stressful time for the bureau, which had to focus on both criminal and national security cases. Through it all, the FBI lacked specific guidelines, from either Congress or the Justice Department, covering investigations of national security threats. Therefore, the FBI went after what it viewed as domestic terror threats from left-wing militants with the bare-knuckle tactics it used against Communists in the 1950s and the KKK in the 1960s. Agents and operatives infiltrated organizations deemed suspect, sowed discord among members, and illegally spied on American citizens. Some of the targets were legitimate threats. Others were civil rights and women's organizations and peaceful antiwar groups. Martin Luther King himself was on the list. Many operations, such as the surveillance of King and efforts to promote violence between black militant groups, were carried out under what was called "Cointelpro," the short name for the Counterintellience Program approved by the National Security Council in 1956 to attack the Communist Party in the United States. It was disbanded by J. Edgar Hoover in 1971 after radicals and some members of Congress exposed it to the public.

Cointelpro was not a major operation compared to other FBI activities. It consumed the time of only two-tenths of 1 percent the FBI's investigations over 15 years. However, in some instances it did violate First Amendment rights and infringed on other liberties. Moreover, the FBI traditionally has had to deal with fears from civil libertarians that it could become a secret police force, even though accountability to Congress would guard against such a trend. Cointelpro stoked such fears because, in some cases, it blurred the line between protecting the public and infringing on its rights.

In 1975 the Senate held hearings on FBI domestic intelligence operations, especially Cointelpro. A year later, then-Attorney General Edward Levi worked out with the FBI a set of guidelines for domestic security operations. The major change it mandated was that only radicals engaging in violence should be investigated. Two years later, Congress passed the Foreign Intelligence and Surveillance Act (FISA). It tightened rules for surveillance and created a court to decide on requests for activities such as wiretapping. These actions were considered necessary to prevent abuses but made the FBI's job much tougher.

Since the attacks of September 11, 2001, the guidelines have been revised several times. FBI agents are now allowed to recruit informants, shadow people, and operate covertly to gather intelligence domestically to assess security threats. Many civil libertarians and some members of Congress have opposed loosening the rules. The FBI has argued that the revisions enable agents to use the same techniques in national security investigations as they do in criminal investigations and foreign intelligence.

WHEN POLICE OFFICERS GO BAD

FBI agents have to be particularly circumspect when it comes to keeping their investigations within the parameters of the law because it is their job to investigate cases in which other law enforcement officers go bad. In July 2009 a former police officer in Memphis, Tennessee, received a life-plus-255-year sentence as a result of an investigation by the FBI in cooperation with the Memphis Police Department's security squad. Arthur Sease IV was convicted earlier in the year of 444 counts of civil rights, narcotics, robbery, and firearms offenses. The civil rights charges stemmed from the fact that Sease and some of his fellow cops—who were also convicted—used their authority to rob suspected drug dealers. Their take was cocaine, marijuana, and cash. The crooked cops would then resell the stolen drugs. The sentence handed down was one of the longest ever imposed for civil rights violations that did not involved the death of a victim, according to My Harrison, the special agent in charge of the FBI's Memphis field office.[5] The aim of the harsh sentence was to demonstrate the severity of rights violations by government employees.[6]

Police brutality also falls under FBI civil rights jurisdiction. Another Tennessee case occurred in Wilson County, near Nashville. In January 2003 a driver named Walter Steven Kuntz was arrested by Lebanon, Tennessee, police for driving under the influence of a controlled substance. They placed him in the Wilson County Sheriff's Office jail. Once in his cell, Kuntz talked incessantly. As a result, he was badly beaten time and again over several hours by two correctional officers. Eight hours after

MODERN SLAVERY

Most victims in human trafficking cases handled by the FBI are women and young girls from Central America and Asian countries. They are almost always forced into the commercial sex industry or domestic servitude. Men and boys are often forced to work as migrant laborers or in restaurants. They are often in the country illegally and threatened with exposure by their captors in order to keep them in line.

Some of the people forced into servitude are American citizens or residents. Many are young runaways, like young women recruited by a man in Alaska who was found guilty of forcing them to work for him as prostitutes. He controlled them by hooking them on cocaine and brainwashing them.

Increasingly, states are passing their own laws against human trafficking. So far almost 30 states have done so. This enables local and state authorities to arrest and prosecute without federal assistance. FBI agents who have experience dealing with human trafficking have helped train local officers to deal with this crime.

he was placed in the cell, he was hospitalized and declared brain-dead. He died a day later.

FBI agents from the Memphis field office were called in to work with the Tennessee Bureau of Investigation on the case. They discovered that officers on the second shift at the jail had been beating prisoners regularly over a two-year period. Five officers were charged in 2004 with conspiring to violate the civil rights of 13 former inmates of the jail, including Kuntz. Sergeant Patrick Marlowe and Officer Gary Hale were charged with causing Kuntz's death by assaulting him and denying him prompt medical attention. Four officers, including Hale, pled guilty and agreed to cooperate with investigators in the case against Marlowe. Marlowe was tried, convicted, and sentenced to life in prison. Other officers involved received lesser prison terms or received probation.

HUMAN TRAFFICKING

There is no greater violation of a person's civil rights than enslaving him or her. The slave trade and forced servitude still exist, even within industrialized Western nations. The centerpiece of the U.S. government's efforts to eliminate human trafficking is the Trafficking Victims Protection Act of 2000, reauthorized in 2005, according to the U.S. Department of Justice.[7] Human trafficking is a main area of investigation by the FBI both in the United States and through legal attaches abroad. People are enslaved for a variety of purposes, typically prostitution or forced labor. A typical case emerged in June 2005, when two young females reported that they had been sexually victimized, physically abused, and deprived of money by a man who owned a modeling and casting company. He had convinced the girls to sign a modeling contract with him, promising big money from fashion magazines and music videos. The cost for his agent's services was $24,000 to be paid back at $450 weekly. After signing, the agent revealed his true purpose. Threatening to kill the girls and their families, he forced them into prostitution and working in adult clubs to repay their debt.

Working with the Atlanta Police Department, FBI agents went after the agent. They found contracts in his vehicle that helped them identify 18 more victims. Once the media reported the story, more victims emerged. The agent was arrested, eventually pled guilty, and was sentenced to 15 years in prison.

Terrorism

Narseal Batiste had big plans, or so he told an Al-Qaeda "representative, with whom he had a secret meeting." He wanted to wage a "full ground war" against the United States in order to "kill all the devils we can." Among his prospective targets were the Sears Tower in Chicago and FBI headquarters in Washington, D.C. The destruction he and his followers would cause, he vowed, "will be just as good or greater than 9/11." Batiste's revelations to the Al-Qaeda operative, really an FBI informant, in February 2006 were part of the evidence that on May 12, 2009, convicted him and four of his accomplices of multiple terrorism charges. The charges included conspiring to wage war on the United States by discussing and planning attacks inside the nation's borders and to provide material support to Al-Qaeda.

Batiste, the leader of the group, had recruited the others. The media dubbed them the "Liberty City Six" after their hometown, a poor suburb of Miami, Florida. During trial, Batiste claimed they never were serous about the plot. Their defense was that they were looking for a payoff of $50,000 for seeming to cooperate as terrorists. The FBI, they charged, had set them up with an elaborate sting. The jury did not agree, except in the case of a sixth man, who was acquitted on all counts.

COUNTERTERRORISM AFTER 9/11

The operation that resulted in the conviction of Batiste and his ring typifies the aggressive counterterrorism philosophy of the FBI since the attacks of September 11, 2001. FBI operations underwent an extensive reorganization and revision to cope with the post-9/11 world of terrorism. Definitions of terrorism can vary according to one's viewpoint. One person's terrorist can be another's freedom fighter. Terrorism is defined in the *Code of Federal Regulations* as "the unlawful use of force or violence against persons or property to intimidate or coerce a government, the civilian population, or any segment thereof, in furtherance of political or social objectives."[1]

The FBI, under existing U.S. counterterrorism policy, considers terrorists criminals and terrorism as a criminal, not military, matter. It may be surprising, but there is no federal law that makes terrorism in itself a crime. Terrorists are investigated and prosecuted under laws already in place. Often, as in other criminal investigations, a terrorist may be involved in several types of crime. One who plans an attack on a government building, for instance, may be selling drugs to finance the plot.

The laws and regulations governing the FBI's approach to fighting terrorism differ according to whether the terrorists operate only within the United States or in any way internationally. The laws regulate the type of investigative tools and intelligence-gathering methods that investigators can use. Domestic terrorism involves people who live and operate in the United States, carrying out criminal activities to further terrorist objectives, without foreign direction or ties. Their targets are the U.S. government or population. Investigations of domestic terrorism are conducted in accordance with the Attorney General Guidelines for Investigations of General Crimes, Racketeering Enterprises, and Domestic Terrorism Enterprises. Investigations of international terrorists fall under different guidelines, those for FBI Foreign Intelligence and Foreign Counterintelligence Investigations. Terrorism is considered international in scope when it occurs across national boundaries or is committed by a person or organization with links to a foreign power or control group. Its targets can be any government or civilian population.[2]

Terrorist-related activities, according to the FBI's way of describing them, are divided into categories. A terrorist incident is a violent act or an act that endangers human life, that violates criminal law, for purposes of terrorism. A suspected terrorist incident is a potential act of terrorism that at the time cannot be linked to a known or suspected terrorist group or person. A terrorism prevention occurs when investigation blocks terrorists from carrying out a violent act.[3]

9/11 OVERHAUL

The director of the FBI on 9/11, Robert Mueller, had been on the job for only a week when the 9/11 attackers struck. With the Robert Hanssen spy scandal and other internal problems afflicting the bureau, Mueller had been saddled with the job of tuning up the way the bureau operated. After the terrorist attacks, it became very clear that the FBI needed a major overhaul.

First of all, however, 9/11 had to be investigated. The FBI mounted the largest investigation in its history. A quarter of all FBI agents and other personnel were plunged into the task. Their job was twofold: to get the facts on 9/11 and to make sure a second attack was not ready to be launched. It was after the tragic fact of the attack, but all of the terrorists who carried it out were identified. Their trails were backtracked and ties to Al-Qaeda proven. There was no immediate second attack.

The FBI had to revise its priorities and operations. It was not enough to meet crises head on. The agency had to have the long-term capability to predict and head off terrorism. Protecting the nation against acts of terrorism before they occur became the bureau's foremost mission. No amount of successful investigations after a terrorist attack struck could replace stopping it in the first place.

Although the FBI had been in the intelligence business for years, its information was fragmented and not shared in an organized fashion. New policies and high-tech information technology improved the situation, as did laws such as the USA PATRIOT Act, which enables intelligence and criminal investigators to share information more freely. In the words of the FBI, "The right hand now knows what the left is doing." Importantly, many of the FBI tools used against crime were brought to bear against terrorists, such as financial experts who follow money trails. The FBI's revised approach to intelligence stresses amassing information, comparing different scraps and pieces of information, and putting them together to create a big picture of threats and potential threats to U.S. security. Improved information technology is a major part of the effort, which has the overriding goal of preventing terrorism rather than reacting to it.

Coordinating fragmented operations has been the key to retooling the FBI. In 2005 a National Security Branch was established within the FBI. It brings together operations such as counterterrorism, counterintelligence, and intelligence under one umbrella. The branch

SPREAD TOO THIN?

Despite its efforts to reform, the FBI has taken some criticism. Among the critics was former New Jersey Governor Thomas Kean. He chaired the 9/11 Commission, which investigated the attacks, the government's response, and made recommendations for the future. Kean in 2006 complained that the FBI had not truly advanced its intelligence capabilities, which the bureau denied.[4]

Many studies were done on the FBI and its response to new challenges. In 2004 the U.S. General Accounting Office said its study was "inconclusive about the effects of the shifts in the FBI's priorities after September 11 on federal efforts to combat drug, white-collar, and violent crime."[5] Since that report, of course, the impact of hard economic times, corporate scandals, and the Mexican drug cartels has placed increasing demands on FBI resources.

A report in 2005 by the Justice Department's Office of the Inspector General noted that the number of FBI agents assigned to bank robberies had been reduced by 30 percent. Officials of the FBI and local law enforcement questioned in the study admitted that the bureau had eased off on bank robbery investigations.[6] The cases that received attention were those in which robbers used extreme measures, such as violence.

Fears that the FBI was being spread too thin were voiced by some members of Congress. Urging more funding for the Department of Justice in June 2009, U.S. Senator Barbara A. Mikulski (D–MD), voiced this worry. She expressed fears that the FBI was being pulled in too many directions. "The FBI is our domestic security agency tasked with keeping us safe from violent crime, but with a growing international role, their resources could be spread too thin."[7]

acts almost like an agency within an agency. Although competition between various federal law enforcement and intelligence agencies may always exist, since 9/11 the FBI and its counterparts have cooperated much more smoothly in counterterrorism and intelligence. One example of such cooperation is the National Counterterrorism Center, established in 2004. Its director reports to both the president of the United States and to the nation's director of intelligence. At the center, security analysts from the FBI and more than a half dozen other agencies work together to assemble the big picture of terrorist threats.

The FBI's Terrorist Screening Center was established in December 2003 as a single database of known or suspected terrorists. It brings together information in various FBI and law enforcement databases. The center also maintains the U.S. government's Terrorism Watchlist, which has been the subject of some controversy (critics claim people who do not deserve to be on the list are sometimes included).

THE LIBERTY CITY SIX

Another example of multiagency cooperation is the FBI Joint Terrorism Task Forces, operating in more than 100 cities scattered across the country. Almost 4,000 members of dozens of agencies, including local police, the military, and federal agencies such as the Department of Agriculture and the CIA, operate under FBI supervision to counter terrorist plots. They chase down leads, gather evidence, make arrests, provide security for special events, carry on training, gather intelligence, and respond to threats in a flash. A National Joint Terrorism Task Force, based deep in the heart of FBI headquarters, coordinates their operations. The national force is made of more than 50 people from 38 government agencies.

The Liberty City Six investigation was the work of the South Florida Joint Terrorism Task Force. Evidence presented by prosecutors described how Batiste and five of his associates took an oath of loyalty to Al-Qaeda and took photos of government buildings as potential targets. They asked the FBI informant for weapons, radios, vehicles, and $50,000 in a case, which in court they claimed they were trying to scam. The jury did not buy the story.

Members of the New York Police Department and the FBI Joint Terrorism Task Force raid a home in North Bergen, New Jersey. The house was suspected to have ties to terrorism suspect Mohamed Hamoud Alessa, who was arrested before getting on a plane at JFK airport. *(John Munson/Star Ledger/Corbis)*

TAKING DOWN TERRORISTS

FBI takedowns of terrorists began even as the nation reeled from the tragedy of 9/11. In case after case, terrorist plots were foiled by agents or evidence was linked to terrorists in custody. Agents use a variety of counterterrorism techniques, including wiretapping, infiltrating terrorist cells, educating the public to alert the authorities to suspicious activities, and informants. Following are just a few examples of major cases broken since September 11, 2001.

Eighteen days after the 9/11 attacks, a sheriff in Washington State, tipped off, found several men taking target practice in a remote area. When the FBI investigated, they found that the men were linked to a ring of international terrorists in Portland, Oregon. The men were training to join Taliban forces in Afghanistan. Six of them were convicted and a seventh killed while fighting in Pakistan.

In December 2003 the notorious British "Shoe Bomber" Richard Reid was subdued by fellow passengers when he tried to set off a bomb hidden in his high-top shoes. An FBI investigation led to his conviction and a life sentence.

The case of the Virginia jihad was finally settled with the sentencing of the last defendant in 2002. It involved a radical cell of men operating in Northern Virginia. They were inspired by and connected to the Pakistan-based Lashkar-e-Taiba, a militant group behind violence in the Indian state of Kashmir. Some of the Virginia cell's members had been to terrorist training camps in Pakistan and planned to return to fight the Americans in Afghanistan. The FBI investigation resulted in the conviction of 11 people on terrorism charges. Other terrorists were arrested abroad as a result of the case.

THE VOLUNTEER WRATH INVESTIGATION

Not all terrorism that threatens the United States comes from Al-Qaeda and other foreign or international groups. There are Americans who would use terrorist tactics to further their own political or social crusades. Such domestic terrorism groups include neo-Nazis as well as

RUBY RIDGE, WACO, AND CRITICAL RESPONSE

Two bloody and disastrous standoffs that occurred in late 1992 and early 1993 rocked the FBI and the federal law enforcement establishment in general. In August 1992 a U.S. marshal and Randy Weaver's 14-year-old son were killed in an exchange of fire at the cabin of Weaver and his family in remote Ruby Ridge, Idaho. Weaver had failed to appear in court on federal weapons charges and was under surveillance by federal officers. In the siege that followed, an FBI sniper accidentally killed Weaver's wife and baby. Weaver was later acquitted on all charges but failed to show up in court. He received a monetary settlement from the federal government. Several FBI officials were disciplined and the bureau admitted its agents had overreacted.

Eight months later, a standoff occurred between agents of the ATF and an armed religious sect called the Branch Davidians at their walled compound outside Waco, Texas. Four agents and six sect members were killed. FBI agents attempted to end the standoff, which lasted 51 days. They shot tear gas into the compound and a fire erupted. Seventy-six Davidians died in the flames. Investigations afterward showed that the FBI had not fired gunshots or used any materials that could have started the fire. The suspected causes of the fire range from arson perpetrated by the Davidians to government gunfire during the assault.

The two tragedies led to the establishment of a new unit within the FBI—the Critical Incident Response Group—that began operating in 1994. The group is designed to respond rapidly to and manage explosive crises. The concept behind the group is to deploy a comprehensive array of tactical and investigative resources at once. It allows unified action by crises negotiators, managers, and logistical experts.

many white supremacist organizations, radical animal rights groups, and some extreme environmental groups. During the years 2002–2005, 23 of the 24 terrorist incidents recorded in the United States were carried out by domestic terrorists.[8] A discontented Tennessee farmer who had been a member of the right-wing National Socialist Movement was one of them. Demetrius Van Crocker regularly spouted his extremist rants to people who knew him. When, in 2004, he began to talk about building a dirty bomb to blow up a state or federal courthouse, someone who took him seriously called the Tennessee Bureau of Investigation. State officials in turn contacted the FBI.

Agents set up an undercover sting by wiring an undercover witness whose conversations with Van Crocker confirmed that he hoped to blow up a courthouse. The witness offered to put Van Crocker in touch with an individual who could provide the explosives and biological weapons to make the bomb. When Van Crocker met the undercover agent, he expressed doubts. "I don't know you," he said. "How do I know I can trust you?" Even so, Van Crocker told the agent he needed sarin, a nerve gas, and C-4 plastic explosives. He gave the agent $500 to supposedly bribe a guard at an Arkansas weapons arsenal to get the materials. When the agent, carrying an inert sarin canister and wrapped plastic explosives, met Van Crocker in a hotel room, FBI agents swarmed. A search of Van Crocker's home found components for making pipe bombs and a cache of loaded weapons. When a jury considered the evidence, it rendered a verdict in 90 minutes. Van Crocker was convicted on five counts of trying to acquire chemical weapons and explosives to destroy government buildings. He was sentenced to 30 years in prison.

ECOTERRORISM

There are right-wing terrorists, left-wing terrorists, Islamic terrorists, narco-terrorists—a host of groups who use terrorism to further their causes. The FBI has added to the list what it calls "special interest terrorism."[9] It differs from the traditional forms of terrorism in that its adherents aim to resolve specific issues, not cause widespread political or social change. These groups, according to the FBI, are on the fringes of causes that are in themselves legitimate, including the pro-life, environmental, and animal rights movements. Of them all, the one that the FBI views as the most dangerous are ecoterrorists, which include some radical animal rights groups. Two of the most extreme groups pinpointed by the FBI are the Animal Liberation Front and Earth Liberation Front.

Since 1979, according to the FBI, ecoterrorists have committed more than 2,000 crimes. They have caused more than $100 million in damage with attacks on lumber companies, animal testing facilities, corporations, and husbandry operations such as mink farms. They have threatened individuals employed by the companies and organizations they target. Arson is among their favorite weapons. All but one of the incidents of domestic terrorism between 2002 and 2005 were committed by special-interest terrorists in the animal rights and environmental movements, according to the FBI.[10]

One of the most publicized convictions on ecoterrorism charges was that of Eric McDavid, 29, of Foresthill, California. He was sentenced in May 2008 to almost 20 years in prison for conspiring to use fire and explosives to attack the Nimbus Dam and fish hatchery, the U.S. Forest Service Institute of Forest Genetics, cell phone towers, electric power stations, and other targets. The FBI made the arrest after using an informant who infiltrated McDavid's group. While in prison, his case was appealed. McDavid became a hero of radical environmental groups, anarchists, vegans, and other fringe groups.

COUNTERINTELLIGENCE

Allied to the FBI's counterterrorism role is its function as the only federal agency mandated to investigate foreign counterintelligence cases within the borders of the United States. The FBI has designated espionage as a priority just below terrorism. Counterintelligence can be defined in the simplest terms as thwarting efforts at espionage, or spying. Working with other federal agencies such as the CIA, the FBI also can investigate espionage cases overseas if the subject is a U.S. citizen.

FBI counterintelligence can involve outright spying by foreign nations, such as occurred in the case of turncoat FBI agent Robert Hanssen. Often, it involves economic espionage, the theft of intellectual property and technology—business trade secrets. The FBI estimates that in the global marketplace, the United States loses billions of dollars to foreign competitors who spy on the nation's industries. They use the same methods as all spies, including gleaning information from the Internet, outright theft of documents, payoffs to insiders, and hiring secret agents. Stealing economic assets often is not simply a crime against the individual or organization that owns them; it can also damage the national economy. If the stolen property involves military technology, it can directly damage national security.

The Economic Espionage Act of 1996, which makes the theft of commercial secrets a federal crime, gives the FBI jurisdiction over such

CYBERSLEUTHS

FBI sleuths also operate in cyberspace. The FBI's Cyber Division has a broad mission. It combats hackers and the spread of computer viruses. Threats to national security from cyber assaults on facilities such as transportation and communications hubs are a very high priority for the FBI. It seeks to identify and stop online sexual predators and eliminate child pornography. Other targets include scam artists, intellectual property thieves, and copyright pirates. Internet fraud by organized criminal operations is also on the list.

The Cyber Division is based at FBI headquarters. It manages investigations of cyber crime and gives technical support to other FBI operation areas such as counterterrorism and criminal investigations. Regional Cyber Action Teams respond to critical situations such as attacks on national computer security. In addition, most FBI field offices have specialized cybersquads of computer experts.

A typical case is that of the "Mytob" and "Zotob" computer worms unleashed in August 2005. The worms disrupted services on computer networks of many companies, including some news organizations. Working with police in Morocco and Turkey, agents at the Cyber Division homed in on the worms and traced them to a Moroccan and a Turkish resident, both young men. Local authorities in both countries arrested the accused hackers.

violations. Two men arrested by FBI agents at San Francisco International Airport in November 2001 were the first convictions under this law. Fei Ye and Ming Zhong had formed a company in China to manufacture and market a computer microprocessor. The device was to be based on technology stolen from two U.S. corporations. When arrested, the two men had the secret information in their possession.[11]

Sometimes, the stolen items are not simply information but physical items, such as high-tech military equipment. Various federal laws prohibit unregulated export of many military items. A Bellevue, Washington, man broke one of these laws when he conspired to export night vision goggles and cameras that ended up in China. The equipment is used by pilots on night flights. Howard Hsy did not obtain the license and written approval from the State Department needed for the shipment. He was arrested by FBI agents, pled guilty, fined $15,000, and was sentenced to two years of probation.[12]

THE FUTURE OF THE FBI

The FBI marked its centennial by stressing that its reason for existence—the need for a national investigative force—has been proven legitimate. While the FBI admits it has been far from perfect, it stresses that the concept has worked. At the same time, the FBI has been adapting to the changing demands of the future. By improving its utilization of technology and its ability to coordinate multiple operations both within its own jurisdiction and in cooperation with other agencies, the FBI looks to build on its reputation as one of the top law enforcement agencies of its kind in the world.

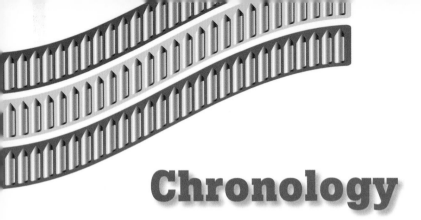

Chronology

1908	**May:** A bill passed by Congress prevents agents from the Secret Service from hiring out to other agencies, thereby stopping the Justice Department from using them for investigations
	June: Attorney General Charles J. Bonaparte orders creation of a special agent force in the Justice Department; 31 investigators form the beginning of the FBI
	July: The formal birth of the FBI occurs when the special agents are told to report to the Justice Department's chief examiner
1909	**March:** The agent force is named the Bureau of Investigation
1917	**April:** Congress declares war on Germany; the president orders the FBI to detain enemy aliens
1924	**May:** J. Edgar Hoover is appointed director of the bureau
	July: The FBI sets up a fingerprint bureau
1925	**October:** An auto thief shoots and kills Special Agent Edwin C. Shanahan, the first agent killed in the line of duty
1932	**June:** The Federal Kidnapping Act gives the bureau authority to investigate kidnappings across state lines
	July: The bureau becomes the United States Bureau of Investigation
	November: The bureau's crime laboratory is opened
1934	**June:** In response to crimes like the Kansas City Massacre, when gangsters killed an agent and other

lawmen, Congress authorizes agents to make arrests and carry firearms

July: John Dillinger dies under agents' gunfire in Chicago

1935   **July:** The bureau becomes the Federal Bureau of Investigation

1939   President Roosevelt assigns the FBI, jointly with military intelligence, to investigate espionage, sabotage, and other subversion

1941   **December:** Within 72 hours of the Japanese attack on Pearl Harbor, the FBI has 3,846 enemy aliens in custody; espionage equipment is also seized

1957   **November:** The Mafia convention at Apalachin, New York, occurs; surveillance and action by the FBI and state law enforcement exposes the nationwide network of organized crime

1963   **June:** Civil rights leader Medgar Evers is killed by Byron De La Beckwith, who is finally found guilty in 1993

November: Lee Harvey Oswald assassinates President John F. Kennedy

1964   **June:** Civil rights workers James E. Chaney, Andrew Goodman, and Michael Schwerner are murdered in Mississippi; the so-called Mississippi Burning case begins

1968   **April:** James Earl Ray assassinates Dr. Martin Luther King Jr.

1970   **October:** Congress approves the Organized Crime Control Act of 1970, which contains the Racketeer Influenced and Corrupt Organization Act (RICO), a powerful tool against organized criminal enterprises

1972   **May:** J. Edgar Hoover dies; new FBI Academy opens at Quantico, Virginia

June: Watergate scandal begins with break-in of Democratic National Committee headquarters

1973   **July:** Clarence M. Kelley becomes FBI director

1978   **February:** William H. Webster becomes FBI director

1981	**January:** Levi guidelines regulate FBI undercover operations
1988	**December:** Pan American 747 carrying 259 people explodes over Lockerbie, Scotland, killing all aboard and 11 on the ground; FBI is involved in investigation of terrorist bombing
1992	**August:** Ruby Ridge shootout with separatist Randy Weaver
1993	**February:** A bomb explodes under the World Trade Center; this first attack kills six people and injures more than 1,000 others; the FBI is involved in investigation; WACO raid at compound of Branch Davidian religious sect leads to 51-day siege and ends with fire that kills 76 sect members.
	September: Louis J. Freeh becomes FBI director
1994	**February:** Agents arrest CIA veteran Aldrich Ames and his wife on charges of spying for the Soviet Union and, later, the Russian Republic
1995	**April:** On the second anniversary of the Waco tragedy, a truck bomb levels the federal building in Oklahoma City; FBI is designated as lead agency in the investigation
1998	**August 7:** Terrorist bombing attacks on U.S. embassies in Kenya and Tanzania bring FBI into investigation
1999	**April 1:** A Taiwanese firm is the first foreign company convicted under the federal Economic Espionage Act of 1996, after FBI investigation
	June: Osama bin Laden added to FBI's Ten Most Wanted fugitives list after charges linked to African embassy bombings
2001	**September:** Robert S. Mueller III becomes FBI Director; World Trade Center/Pentagon attacks occur a week later; 7,000 FBI agents put on the case
	December: Enron case emerges; FBI establishes Office of Law Enforcement Coordination

2005	**February:** National Security Branch established within FBI to coordinate counterterrorism and counterintelligence
	June: Edgar Ray Killen sentenced to 60 years for manslaughter in the Mississipi Burning case
2009	**February:** FBI Director Robert Mueller testifies before Congress that mortgage fraud is mounting at an astonishing rate
	June 29: Financier Bernard Madoff sentenced to 150 years in jail for perpetrating one of the largest Ponzi schemes in history

Endnotes

Introduction

1. U.S. Department of Justice, *Bureau of Justice Statistics Bulletin,* "Federal Law Enforcement Officers, 2004," http://bjs.ojp.usdoj.gov/content/pub/pdf/fleo04.pdf (Accessed August 1, 2009).

Chapter 1

1. 1995 Congressional Hearings Intelligence and Security, *Opening Statement of Louis J. Freeh, Director Federal Bureau of Investigation,* http//:www.fas.org/irp/congress/1995_hr/s951019f.htm (Accessed August 19, 2009).
2. Federal Bureau of Investigation, "The Top Ten Myths in FBI History," *Federal Bureau of Investigation Headline Archives,* http://www.fbi.gov/page2/july08/myths_072408.html (Accessed July 15, 2010).
3. Federal Bureau of Investigation, "About Us-Quick Facts," http://www.fbi.gov/quickfacts.htm (Accessed August 17, 2009).
4. Federal Bureau of Investigation, *Today's FBI Facts and Figures, 2008–2009,* Federal Bureau of Investigation, http://www.fbi.gov/facts_and_figures/fact_and_figures.htm.
5. Federal Bureau of Investigation, "Robert S. Mueller, III Director Federal Bureau of Investigation, Statement Before the Senate Judiciary Committee, March 25, 2009," Federal Bureau of Investigation, http://www.fbi.gov/congress/congress09/mueller032509.htm (Accessed July 15, 2010).
6. Federal Bureau of Investigation, "About Us-Quick Facts," http://www.fbi.gov/quickfacts.htm (Accessed August 17, 2009).

Chapter 2

1. Federal Bureau of Investigation, *The FBI: A Centennial History, 1908–2008,* http://www.fbi.gov/book.htm (Accessed July 14, 2010).
2. Michael Newton, *Criminal Investigations, Gangs and Gang Crime,* (New York: Chelsea House, 2008).
3. Federal Bureau of Investigation, *Lessons at Little Bohemia,* "FBI Raid at Little Bohemia," Federal Bureau of Investigation, http://www.fbi.gov/multimedia/bohemia042309/transcript.htm (Accessed July 15, 2010).
4. Federal Bureau of Investigation, National Academy, Quantico Virginia, "Session 211 (Sept. 2002 to Dec. 2002)," http://www.fbina211.org (Accessed July 15, 2010).
5. Federal Bureau of Investigation, "About Us, Heraldry of the Seal," Federal Bureau of Investigation,

http://www.fbi.gov/libref/historic/
fbiseal/fbiseal.htm (Accessed July
15, 2010).

Chapter 3

1. Federal Bureau of Investigation,
"The Birth of the FBI's Technical
Laboratory, 1924 to 1935" Federal
Bureau of Investigation Office of
Public Affairs, http://www.fbi.gov/
libref/historic/history/birthtechlab.
htm (Accessed July 15, 2010).
2. Ibid.
3. Federal Bureau of Investigation,
*The FBI Laboratory 2007 Annual
Report*, Federal Bureau of Investigation, http://www.fbi.gov/hq/
lab/lab2007/labannual07.htm
(Accessed July 17, 2009).
4. Federal Bureau of Investigation,
"Covering all the Angles," *Federal
Bureau of Investigation Headline
Archives*, http://www.fbi.gov/
page2/dec08/bullets_121208.html
(Accessed July 15, 2010).
5. Federal Bureau of Investigation,
"Bodies of Evidence," http://www
.fbi.gov/page2/july09/bodyfarm
_070709.html (Accessed July 15,
2010).
6. Minutes of the Senate Committee on Judiciary, Seventy-fourth
Session, April 19, 2007 (Nevada),
http://www.leg.state.nv.us/74th/
Minutes/Senate/JUD/Final/980.
pdf (Accessed July 17, 2009).

Chapter 4

1. Federal Bureau of Investigation, FBI History, "History of
the FBI, World War II Period:
1930s–1940s," http://www.fbi.gov/
libref/historic/history/worldwar.
htm. (Accessed July 23, 2009).
2. Federal Bureau of Investigation,
The FBI: A Centennial History,
1908–2008, http://www.fbi.gov/
book.htm (Accessed July 14, 2010).
3. Federal Bureau of Investigation,
The FBI: A Centennial History,
1908–2008, http://www.fbi.gov/
fbihistorybook.htm (Accessed July
15, 2010).
4. Art Ronnie, *Counterfeit Hero: Fritz
Duquesne, Adventurer and Spy*
(Annapolis, Md.: Naval Institute
Press, 1995).
5. Federal Bureau of Investigation, FBI History, Famous Cases,
"George John Dasch and the Nazi
Saboteurs," http://www.fbi.gov/
libref/historic/famcases/nazi/nazi.
htm (Accessed July 15, 2010).
6. Ibid.

Chapter 5

1. National Security Agency (NSA),
VENONA Archives, "Introductory
History of VENONA and Guide
to the Translations," NSA, http://
www.theblackvault.com/docu
ments/nsa/venona/monographs/
monograph-1.html (Accessed July
27, 2009).
2. National Security Agency, Robert
L. Benson, "The VENONA Story,"
http://www.nsa.gov/about/_files/
cryptologic_heritage/publica-
tions/coldwar/venona_story.pdf
(Accessed July 27, 2009).
3. U.S. Department of Justice, Office
of the Inspector General, *A Review
of the FBI's Performance in Deter-
ring, Detecting, and Investigating
the Espionage Activities of Robert
Philip Hanssen*, http://www.justice.
gov/oig/special/0308/index.htm
(Posted August 14, 2003)
4. U.S. Department of Justice, Commission for Review of FBI Security
Programs March 2002, *A Review
of FBI Security Programs,* http://

www.fas.org/irp/agency/doj/fbi/
websterreport.pdf (Accessed July
27, 2009).

5. U.S. Department of Justice, Commission for Review of FBI Security
Programs March 2002, *A Review of
FBI Security Programs,* http://
www.fas.org/irp/agency/doj/fbi/
websterreport.pdf (Accessed July
27, 2009).

6. U.S. Department of Justice, Office
of the Inspector General, *A Review
of the FBI's Performance in Deter-
ring, Detecting, and Investigating
the Espionage Activities of Robert
Philip Hanssen,* http://www.justice.
gov/oig/special/0308/index.htm
(Accessed July 15, 2010).

Chapter 6

1. Federal Bureau of Investigation,
"Turning Point, Using Intel to Stop
the Mob," Federal Bureau of Investigation Headline Archives, www.
fbi.gov/page2/august07/mobin-
tel080907.htm (Accessed July 15,
2010).

2. Federal Bureau of Investigation, *Organized Crime,* "Glos-
sary," http://www.fbi.gov/hq/cid/
orgcrime/glossary.htm (Accessed
August 10, 2009).

3. Ibid.

4. Federal Bureau of Investigation,
"About Organized Crime," http://
www.fbi.gov/hq/cid/orgcrime/
aboutocs.htm (Accessed July 29,
2009).

5. Martin Roth, *The Writer's Complete Crime Reference Book* (Cin-
cinnati, Ohio: Writers Digest
Books, 1993).

6. 1996 Congressional Hearings,
Intelligence and Security, "State-
ment of Louis J. Freeh, Director,
Federal Bureau of Investigation,

Before the House Committee on
International Relations, Hearing
on Russian Organized Crime, April
30, 1996," http://www.fas.org/irp/
congress/1996_hr/h960430f.htm
(Accessed July 15, 2010).

Chapter 7

1. Federal Bureau of Investigation,
"In Search of D.B. Cooper, New
Developments in the Unsolved
Case," Federal Bureau of Investi-
gation Headline Archives, http://
www.fbi.gov/page2/march09/
dbcooper031709.html (Accessed
July 15, 2010).

2. Federal Bureau of Investigation,
"Famous Cases: John Dillinger,"
http://www.fbi.gov/libref/historic/
famcases/dillinger/dillinger.htm
(Accessed July 15, 2010.

3. Federal Bureau of Investigation,
*The FBI: A Centennial History,
1908–2008,* Federal Bureau of
Investigation, http://www.fbi.gov/
fbihistorybook.htm (Accessed July
15, 2010).

4. Federal Bureau of Investigation,
"Crime on the High Seas, Cruises
not a Vacation from Vigilance,"
*Federal Bureau of Investigation
Headline Archives,* http://www.
fbi.gov/page2/may06/cruise_
crime052206.htm (Accessed July
15, 2010).

5. Federal Bureau of Investigation, "Crimes Against Children,"
Federal Bureau of Investigation,
http://www.fbi.gov/hq/cid/cac/
family.htm (Accessed August 10,
2009).

6. Federal Bureau of Investigation,
"Forty-Eight Children Recovered
in Operation Cross Country III,"
Federal Bureau of Investigation
Press Release, http://www.fbi.gov/

pressrel/pressrel09/crosscountry_
022309.htm (Accessed July 15,
2010).

Chapter 8

1. U.S. Department of Justice,
"Congressman William Jefferson
Indicted on Bribery, Racketeering,
Money Laundering, Obstruction
of Justice, and Related Charges,"
U.S. Department of Justice Press
Release, http://www.justice.gov/
opa/pr/2009/August/09-crm-775.
html (Accessed July 15, 2010).
2. Federal Bureau of Investigation,
Robert S. Mueller III Congressional Testimony, "Statement Before
the House Judiciary Committee,"
Federal Bureau of Investigation,
http://www.fbi.gov/congress/
congress09/mueller052009.htm
(Accessed July 15, 2010).
3. Ibid.
4. Federal Bureau of Investigation, "More than 400 Defendants
Charged for Roles in Mortgage
Fraud Schemes as Part of Operation 'Malicious Mortgage,'" Federal
Bureau of Investigation Press
Release, http://www.fbi.gov/
pressrel/pressrel08/mortgage-
fraud061908.htm (Accessed July
15, 2010).
5. Federal Bureau of Investigation,
"Robert S. Mueller III Congressional Testimony, Statement Before
the House Judiciary Committee,
Federal Bureau of Investigation,"
http://www.fbi.gov/congress/
congress09/mueller052009.htm
(Accessed July 15, 2010).
6. "'Evil' Madoff Gets 150 Years in
Epic Fraud," The Wall Street Journal, http://online.wsj.com/article/
SB124604151653862301.html
(Accessed July 15, 2010).

Chapter 9

1. Federal Bureau of Investigation,
"A Byte Out of History, Mississippi Burning," Federal Bureau of
Investigation Headline Archives,
http://www.fbi.gov/page2/feb07/
miburn022607.htm (Accessed July
15, 2010).
2. Federal Bureau of Investigation,
"Summary of the Investigation
of the 1964 murder of three civil
rights workers near Philadelphia,
Mississippi," http://foia.fbi.gov/
foiaindex/miburn.htm (Accessed
July 15, 2010).
3. Federal Bureau of Investigation,
"Cold Case Initiative, Seeking
Information on More than 100
Civil Rights-Era Murders," Federal
Bureau of Investigation Headline
Archives, http://www.fbi.gov/
page2/feb09/coldcases022609.html
(Accessed July 15, 2010).
4. Federal Bureau of Investigation,
The FBI: A Centennial History,
1908–2008, http://www.fbi.gov/
book.htm (Accessed July 14,
2010).
5. U.S. Department of Justice, U.S.
Attorney's Office, Western District
of Tennessee, "Former Memphis
Police Officer Sentenced to Prison
Terms of Life Plus 255 Years for
Civil Rights, Narcotics, Robbery,
and Firearms Crimes," Federal
Bureau of Investigation Press
Release, http://memphis.fbi.gov/
dojpressrel/pressrel09/me070109.
htm (Accessed July 15, 2010).
6. Ibid.
7. U.S. Department of Justice, Attorney General's Annual Report to
Congress and Assessment of the
U.S. Government Activities to Com-
bat Trafficking in Persons Fiscal
Year 2007, http://www.justice.gov/

archive/ag/annualreports/tr2007/
agreporthumantrafficking2007.pdf
(Accessed July 15, 2010).

Chapter 10

1. Federal Bureau of Investigation,
   Terrorism 2000/2001, http://
   www.fbi.gov/publications/terror/
   terror2000_2001.htm (Accessed
   August 20, 2009).
2. Federal Bureau of Investigation,
   "Testimony of James F. Jarboe,
   Domestic Terrorism Section Chief,
   Counterterrorism Division, FBI,
   Before the House Resources Committee, Subcommittee on Forests
   and Forest Health, February 12,
   2002, The Threat of Eco-Terror-
   ism," Federal Bureau of Investigation, http://www.fbi.gov/congress/
   congress02/jarboe021202.htm
   (Accessed July 15, 2010).
3. Federal Bureau of Investigation,
   Terrorism 2000/2001, http://
   www.fbi.gov/publications/terror/
   terror2000_2001.htm (Accessed
   August 20, 2009).
4. Allen Levin and Kevin Johnson,
   "9/11Panel Heads: FBI Lags on
   Promised Improvements," *USA
   Today*, August 17, 2006.
5. U.S. General Accounting Office,
   *FBI Transformation: Data Incon-
   clusive on Effects of Shift to Coun-
   terterrorism-Related Priorities on
   Traditional Crime Enforcement*,
   General Accounting Office, http://
   www.gao.gov/htext/d041036.html
   (Accessed August 11, 2009).
6. U.S. Department of Justice, Office
   of the Attorney General, *The
   External Effects of the Federal
   Bureau of Investigation's Repri-
   oritization Efforts, September
   2005, Office of the Attorney Gen-*

eral, http://www.justice.gov/oig/
reports/FBI/a0537/chapter8.htm
(Accessed August 17, 2009).
7. Senator Barbara Mikulski, "Chair-
   woman Mikulski Makes Community Security a Priority in
   Federal Checkbook," Press Release,
   http://mikulski.senate.gov/record.
   cfm?id=315038 (Posted June 24,
   2009).
8. Federal Bureau of Investigation,
   Terrorism 2002-2005, http://www.
   fbi.gov/publications/terror/terror-
   ism2002_2005.htm (Accessed July
   15, 2010).
9. Federal Bureau of Investigation,
   "Testimony of James F. Jarboe,
   Domestic Terrorism Section Chief,
   Counterterrorism Division, FBI,
   Before the House Resources Committee, Subcommittee on Forests
   and Forest Health, February 12,
   2002, The Threat of Eco-Terror-
   ism," http://www.fbi.gov/congress/
   congress02/jarboe021202.htm
   (Accessed July 15, 2010).
10. Federal Bureau of Investigation,
    Terrorism 2002-2005, Federal
    Bureau of Investigation, http://
    www.fbi.gov/publications/ter-
    ror/terrorism2002_2005.htm
    (Accessed July 15, 2010).
11. United States Department of Jus-
    tice, "Two Men Plead Guilty to
    Stealing Trade Secrets from Sili-
    con Valley Companies to Benefit
    China," http://www.justice.gov/
    criminal/cybercrime/yePlea.htm
    (Accessed July 15, 2010).
12. Federal Bureau of Investiga-
    tion, "Today's FBI: Investigative
    Programs," http://www.fbi.gov/
    facts_and_figures/investiga-
    tive_programs.htm (Accessed July
    15, 2010).

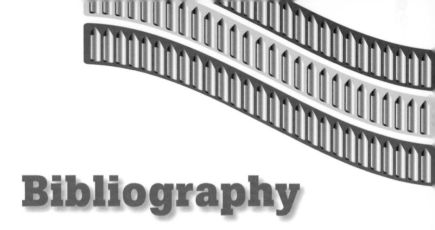

Bibliography

Federal Bureau of Investigation. "Terrorism 2002–2005." Available online. URL: http://www.fbi.gov/publications/terror/terrorism2002_2005.htm. Accessed July 15, 2010.

Federal Bureau of Investigation. "The FBI: A Centennial History, 1908–2008." Available online. URL: http://www.fbi.gov/fbihistorybook.htm. Accessed July 15, 2010.

Federal Bureau of Investigation. "Today's FBI 2008–2009." Available online. URL: http://www.fbi.gov/facts_and_figures/fact_and_figures.htm. Accessed July 15, 2010.

Kelly, Robert J., Jess Maghan, and Joseph D. Serio. *Illicit Trafficking: A Reference Handbook*. Santa Barbara: ABC-CLIO, 2005.

Maas, Peter. *Underboss*. New York: HarperCollins, 1997.

Ricciuti, Edward. *Science 101: Forensics*. New York: HarperCollins, 2007.

Vise, David A. *The Bureau and the Mole*. New York: Atlantic Monthly Press, 2002.

Weiss, Murray. *The Man Who Warned America*. New York: Regan Books, 2003.

Further Resources

Print

Federal Bureau of Investigation. *FBI Handbook of Crime Scene Forensics.* New York: Skyhorse Press, 2008. The official guide for law enforcement submitting evidence to the FBI. Proper methods for investigating crime scenes. Interesting reading for lay people.

Federal Bureau of Investigation. *Handbook of Forensic Services.* (Available to law enforcement in field-manual format from the FBI Laboratory, Quantico, Virginia.) May be viewed online at http://www.fbi.gov/hq/lab/handbook/forensics.pdf. Technical but easily read. Behind-the-scenes science secrets.

O'Brien, Susan. *Child Abduction and Kidnapping.* New York: Chelsea House, 2008. The history and state of child abductions and what law enforcement is doing to combat these crimes.

Multimedia

The FBI: Legacy and Legends
The FBI: A Century of Excellence
Videos produced by the Society of Former Special Agents of the FBI. Inspirational productions of interesting and sometimes dramatic stills with a musical background. Legacy and Legends focuses largely on the FBI against terrorism and changes in the agency after the attacks of September 11, 2001. A Century of Excellence covers the history of the FBI, ranging from the pursuit of gangsters during the 1930s to scientific crime fighting today.

Online

FBI Official Web Site
http://www.fbi.gov
The entryway to a vast number of FBI documents and audiovisual productions. News and current events, history—everything about the FBI.

Index

About the Author

Edward R. Ricciuti is author of more than 80 books and has written thousands of periodical articles in a career spanning almost 50 years. His books include *Forensics 101*, *Wildlife Special Agent*, and the *Snake Almanac*. Ricciuti's assignments have taken him around the world. He has been in the field with law enforcement agencies here and abroad. He has reported from places as diverse as the imperial palace of the Shah of Iran, the headquarters of the South African Police (SAP), the world's first private undersea laboratory, scientific base camps on the African savanna, the war zone in the former Yugoslavia, and a High Andes police post in the heart of Peru's Shining Path country.

Ricciuti cut his teeth as a newspaper reporter on local police beats in New York and New Jersey. He wrote about a full range of crime, from bank robberies to murders. He graduated to covering major stories on organized crime, urban riots, Soviet spying, and industrial espionage. A graduate of the University of Notre Dame, Ricciuti was a Sloan-Rockefeller Advanced Science Writing Fellow at the Columbia University Graduate School of Journalism and a curator at the New York Zoological Society. He combined his expertise in science, nature and conservation with his crime reporting background to regularly investigate and report on the international illegal trade in wildlife.